For me, joy in hard times is great evidence fo[...] a contagious life. Through the years Phil's sto[...] and deeply ponder things that really matter. I[...]

—**Lee Strobel,** *New York Times* bestselling author

Phil Callaway is a steward of stories, humor, and pain. He seasons our lives with joy and laughter drawn from the deep well of living. Splash through this book and see if you're not refreshed. I double-dog dare you.

—**Chris Fabry,** *New York Times* bestselling author and host of *Chris Fabry Live*

If Phil Callaway was just another old funny guy, he wouldn't be so cool. The fact that he combines humor and relevant spiritual truth in a winsome way makes reading him a pleasure, kind of like consuming a great vitamin hidden inside a raspberry Gummi Bear.

—**Ellen Vaughn,** *New York Times* bestselling author

Phil Callaway can find something to laugh about almost anywhere—he could probably make hitting your own funny bone funny. But he's no mere jokester. He's wise more than wisecracking. Yes, he sees the comedy of errors that makes up much of life, but here's the best part: he sees it, not with scorn or sarcasm, but with love. A comedian can make you laugh. Only a true humorist can make you cry as well, and for all the right reasons. Phil is a true humorist, and—frankly—one of the best.

—**Mark Buchanan,** author of *GodSpeed* and *The Rest of God*

Laugh Like a Kid Again will make you do exactly that. Better yet, Phil's genius in writing is that he makes you laugh while you swallow a compelling chunk of otherwise difficult truth. You'll love this read.

—**Carl Medearis,** author of *Muslims, Christians, and Jesus*

I once got one of Callaway's jokes an hour after I heard him speak. I was on an elevator. I laughed so hard people thought I was crazy. It won't take you an hour to get his humor. This book crackles with insight and wit. It sizzles with the wisdom of one who has faced pain and discovered contagious joy. This should be called *Have a New Laugh by Friday*.

—**Dr. Kevin Leman,** *New York Times* bestselling author of *Have a New Kid by Friday*

Reading Phil Callaway's fantastic new book, I kept thinking of a quote attributed to Oliver Wendell Holmes, Jr.: "I would not give a fig for the simplicity this side of complexity, but I would give my life for the simplicity on the other side of complexity." Substitute the word "laughter" for the word "simplicity" and you'll get what I mean. Phil offers the kind of deep, cleansing laughter you can only find on the far side of real-life complexity—laughter tenderized by tragedy, seasoned by experience, and grounded in faith. I can't recommend *Laugh Like a Kid Again* more highly. I give it five out of five figs!"

—**Carolyn Arends,** recording artist, speaker, author, and Renovaré director of education

Loved it! I couldn't stop laughing. My wife asked what was so funny. I read a single paragraph. She laughed so hard her sides hurt, but her headache's gone. Results may vary. You're duly warned!

—**David Sanford,** author, fan since 1989 (Phil's first *Servant* article), addict since 1993 (Phil's first book)

I couldn't put this book down. Phil has an uncanny way of finding what's funny in life and using it to get talking about things that matter most. Read it and be inspired!

—**Carmen Imes,** author of *Bearing God's Name*, New Testament professor at Prairie College

Phil Callaway is one of the funniest guys I know, and once again, he doesn't disappoint. His Hawaii story alone is worth the price of admission. *Laugh Like a Kid Again* doesn't just serve up laughs but also a much-needed dish of poignancy.

—**Mike Yorkey,** coauthor of *The Shot Caller* and one of Phil's golf buddies

While I was reading this book, geese tromped up and down my arms and waddled across the back of my neck leaving proverbial bumps in their wake. We learn best when our minds are open, our hearts are wide and our lungs are filled with uproarious delight. Phil says, "May we spend more time looking up than looking back." I'm definitely "up" for that.

—**B.J. Taylor,** author of *Charlie Bear*, *Guideposts* writer, and prolific *Chicken Soup for the Soul* contributor

Phil Callaway understands something about Jesus that few others do—He's really, really funny, because He invented that whole humor thing. Phil is a master at whisking together the water-and-oil of grief and laughter. These stories are vivid, visceral, and unforgettable. You will "taste and see" the raw beauty of God's heart when you least expect it.

—**Rick Lawrence,** editor of the *Jesus-Centered Bible* and author of *The God Who Fights for You*

A lifeline of happiness! Humor is the towrope that raises us out of the waves onto the wakeboard of life—and Phil Callaway is a high-powered motor boat of hilarity that will help you giggle, chuckle—even laugh out loud for joy.

—**Pam and Bill Farrel,** authors of *Men Are Like Waffles, Women Are Like Spaghetti* and *Red-Hot Monogamy*

Laugh like a Kid Again

PHIL CALLAWAY

HARVEST HOUSE PUBLISHERS
EUGENE, OREGON

Cover design by Studio Gearbox

Cover photo © Amy Covington / Stocksy ; Wildfloweret / Shutterstock

For bulk, special sales, or ministry purposes, please call 1-800-547-8979.
Email: customerservice@hhpbooks.com

This book contains stories in which people's names and some details of their stories have been changed to protect their privacy.

Laugh like a Kid Again
Copyright © 2020 by Phil Callaway
Published by Harvest House Publishers
Eugene, Oregon 97408
www.harvesthousepublishers.com

ISBN 978-0-7369-7829-3 (pbk.)
ISBN 978-0-7369-7830-9 (eBook)

Library of Congress Cataloging-in-Publication Data is on file at the Library of Congress, Washington, DC.

Printed in the United States of America

20 21 22 23 24 25 26 27 28 / BP-SK / 10 9 8 7 6 5 4 3 2 1

Contents

Part 3: Leave Footsteps Worth Following

To our loyal *Laugh Again* audience—
even the guy who shook my hand and said,
"I listen to you every day on the radio.
I had an image of you in my mind.
Um, uh, I prefer that image."

Thanks for your encouragement,
prayers, and comments.

Most of them.

The Journey Back

When I was four, I told my mother, "I wanna grow up and be a comedian."

She thought about that and said, "Well, Son, you can't do both."

She was right. You can't grow up and do what I do. Each day I go looking for something that will deliver a shot of hope and a smidge of joy to those who read my books and tune in to the radio show *Laugh Again*.

I couldn't know how badly Mom would need that hope. Abused as a child, she spent an excessive amount of my boyhood "sick." That's what they called it back then. I'm told I would bounce into her bedroom, Tigger-like, and say funny things and make funny faces—anything to coax a smile. If I got it right, she would giggle, crawl out of bed, and make me lunch. It was my first paying gig, I suppose.

Laughter is good medicine for the depressed and anxious. The science on this is airtight. But in time I discovered firsthand that as great a gift as laughter is, the more we age, the more elusive it becomes.

I sometimes ask audiences, "How many of you have been doing

too much laughing lately?" In a crowd of three hundred, just one or two hands go up. If kids are present, most put both hands in the air, then look at their parents to see if they'll be sentenced to a time-out. Of course, they don't have jobs yet, or spouses, or deadlines, or in-laws, or mortgages, or Facebook, or dead skunks in their trunks (long story). We all love to find laughter, but life has a way of hiding it from us.

When our kids were small, my wife, Ramona, was tested for Huntington's disease, a fatal hereditary disorder. Three of her siblings had been diagnosed with it. Grand mal seizures were taking hold of her. Every half hour. I was a comedian, but laughter vanished from our home. Bitterness arrived. This lethal companion yanked us into a downward spiral. The journey back was a long one. We're still on it.

One night after I spoke somewhere, a young woman came to me and lifted her denim sleeve. Crisscrossing her wrist were scars, some of them fresh. "I wouldn't be alive if it weren't for the message God has given you," she said. "Would you put it in a book? Please?" For her, laughter was a windshield wiper. It hadn't stopped the rain, but it allowed her to keep going.

More than anything, my relationship with Jesus of Nazareth has kept me going. I'm not a preacher like my dad, but you'll likely hear him whispering in these pages.

Folks call me a humorist, which means, I suppose, that certain paragraphs may make you laugh, and others may cause your eyes to leak a little. I hope that's okay. I've prefaced each chapter with a stand-up joke. Some should make you laugh. The puns should make you wince.

These stories were written along a busted road strewn with speed bumps that threatened to launch me skyward and potholes that threatened to swallow me whole. Some took shape after sitting with my best friend, Lauren, as bone cancer did its thing. They were written for Jeff, who said, "I've been freakin' out lately. Have you watched the news?" For Alan, who has been crippled by anxiety and imprisoned in a psych ward. For Angie, whose husband battles early-onset dementia. And for those like Jesse, who told me, "I haven't laughed since the accident. It's been three years. Tonight I did. Tonight you got me hoping that maybe there's hope." These stories are for those who tell me exactly when the joy left, then ask if it can ever return. My answer is yes, of course.

I pray this book will be a life-giving companion on your journey to joy. I hope it helps you laugh like a kid again. And I promise to keep it brief.

As Henry the VIII told his fifth wife, Catherine, "I won't be keeping you long."

Part 1

Lighten Up a Little

 I know life can be strange, but imagine
being the very first guy to hear a parrot talk.

told a joke on the radio about a single lady who specified that at her funeral there be no male pallbearers. "They wouldn't take me out when I was alive," she said, "I don't want 'em taking me out when I'm dead."

On my desk is a three-page letter telling me off. It's beautifully written. But there's no return address. "You're just one more voice mocking single people," it says. Well, actually, I'm not. I'm a guy with close single friends, all of whom find this joke hilarious.[1]

I think some of us need to loosen our shorts a notch or two. Half the population is full-time offended. They have no formal training, just a doctorate from the Department of Offense (DOO) which they received by mailing in two Corn Flakes Box Tops and a self-addressed, stamped envelope. I think they want us to be as miserable as they are. And the future will be mighty cloudy with these people in charge.

I once told of five-year-old Chrissy, who climbed onto Grandpa's knee and said, "Can you make a noise like a frog?"

Grandpa asked, "Why?"

"Because," said Chrissy, "Daddy said that when you croak we can all go to Disneyland."

Someone told me, "There's nothing funny about death. I'm sorry you think there is."

I was speechless. Few people my age have been to as many funerals as I have, thanks to Huntington's disease and cancer and a host of other unwelcome guests. Yet, in the midst of it all, the hope of heaven keeps me leaning forward. Laughter helps too.

But how can we laugh when times are hard and people disappoint? How can we lighten up when storms threaten and anxiety reigns?

May these stories remind us that we are loved unreasonably, that we are in good hands, that God has always done amazing things in the dark.

Our mouths were filled with laughter,
our tongues with songs of joy.
Then it was said among the nations,
"The LORD has done great things for them."
PSALM 126:2 NIV

1

What Tornado?

 Do you ever worry? I worry that the guy who invented the singing fish is out there working on something new.

Do not needlessly endanger your lives;
wait until I give you the signal.
GENERAL DWIGHT D. EISENHOWER

N o way! Unbelievable!" Steve yelled, dropping his jaw and a fistful of cherries. He was standing by our dining room table, staring out the northwest window, shocked.

We live on the edge of a quiet town. Population 4,000—if you count cats. Little happens here. Until that June day when our son was visiting. Could it be? A towering tornado appeared to be moving in the general direction of our house. It's hard to tell exactly where tornadoes are headed, so Steve did what any responsible male adult would do. He grabbed his smartphone, threw open the back door, and ran straight toward the beast in hopes of a better camera angle.

The monster touched down a mile from our house and began sucking up dirt and bushes and cows. The cows came raining down on our town, crashing through rooftops. It was a cowpocalypse.

Okay, I'm kidding about the cows. But the rest is true. The tornado kept coming. Steve's mother hollered, "Get inside. Think of your wife, your children." But the boy kept calm and filmed on, capturing breathtaking footage.

Remarkably, no cows or humans were injured. One woman broke her arm scrambling to get into her basement, but that was it. A roof was torn from a barn, a grain bin was hurled half a mile, and an RV was flipped and crumpled. Meanwhile, half the town pointed their phones at the sky and gasped, "Whoa! Did you ever in all your life?"

And then there was Theunis Wessels. Theunis and his wife, Cecilia, live a dozen doors east of us. They moved from South Africa recently to settle on the north edge of a town where little happens.

When the twister landed, they had front-row seats. But Cecilia was napping. And Theunis? Well, he had things to do.

Their daughter woke Cecilia by yelling, "Mommy, look!" Mommy rushed to the window. A massive tornado ripped through the field behind their house while her husband calmly mowed the lawn.

Like my son, her first thought was, *Grab a camera!* "I took the picture to show my mum and dad in South Africa," she later told reporters. "And now everyone is like, 'Why is your husband mowing the lawn?'"[1]

"I had to get it cut," Theunis told reporters. A lot was happening over the weekend. A storm was coming. "So I had to make sure I got it done."[2] Was he aware that the tornado was there? "Oh yes," he said. "But I was keeping an eye on it."[3]

Cecilia posted the picture on social media, and it went viral. The BBC, CNN, and *Time* were among the hundreds captivated by the picture and story. Photoshop gurus superimposed Theunis on disaster posters: *The Titanic. The Hindenburg. Godzilla. Star Wars.* A German news outlet labeled him "the Chuck Norris of lawn mowing."[4] Others called him a "super-dad." *The Washington Times* dubbed him "a breathtaking Internet legend."[5]

Lawn mower man: Theunis Wessels on a breezy Friday afternoon. The media frenzy soon died down, but not before the photo was featured in *Vice*, a biopic of former US vice president Dick Cheney. It was used during a scene when Cheney decides how to proceed following the terrorist attacks on September 11, 2001. Cecilia Wessels says, "I really want to thank my daughter for waking me up so I could take this photo. Otherwise this all would have never happened."

Theunis laughed and shrugged his shoulders. "[The tornado] looks much closer if you look in the photo," he said, "but it was really far away. Well, not really far, far away, but it was far away from us."[6]

Some think Theunis is crazier than a four-dollar bill. Not me. I like this guy. Now, should you take cover if a tornado is coming? Yes. Absolutely. Please do. But the photo reminds me of a tiny bird perched on a nest while a thundering waterfall misses it by inches. It reminds me of the storms that enter all our lives. Soldiers deployed overseas contacted Theunis and Cecilia. When facing the worst, the photo spoke to them of the courage they needed to carry on.

I asked Theunis about storms. "I've had my share," he said. One hit when he was leading a pack climbing Russia's highest peak. "I slipped and fell 100 meters downward. They evacuated me just 200 meters short of reaching the summit. That was a lifelong dream. Maybe that tornado prepared me for this one."

Then he told me his secret. It's the part of his story the papers and TV shows didn't tell. "If your heart and soul belong to God," he said, "storms still come. We still ask, 'Why does this happen to us?' We don't know. But we know one day we will find out. So keep your faith. You're in his hands. Trust God and be faithful."

Or as someone said on Twitter, "When the going gets tough, the tough get mowing."[7]

2

Dog Gone

 We love our dog, but she's not the smartest on the block. She cost us $400. That's $100 per brain cell.

In loving me, you made me lovable.

SAINT AUGUSTINE

My mother sang me nursery rhymes when I was younger—to prepare me for the perils of life, I suppose. Nursery rhymes in which Little Bo-Peep lost her sheep, three blind mice lost their tails, and Humpty Dumpty lost his balance and was never able to pull himself together again. I listened as weasels went *pop*, cradles went *crash*, and an old man went to bed and bumped his head and staggered around singing, "Twinkle, Twinkle, Little Star."

One song in particular depressed the life out of me.

I lost my kitty, my poor little kitty,
I wandered the fields all 'round.
I looked in the cradle and under the table,
But nowhere could kitty be found.
So I took my hook, and went to the brook,
To see if my kitty was there.

But there I found that she had been drowned,
And so I gave up in despair.

Mom sang this softly to me, kissed my forehead, then said, "Okay. Off to bed, Son. Have a good sleep."

When I had children of my own, I came up with a happier ending:

So I took my hook and went down to the brook,
To see if she'd gotten that far.
I say unattested that she'd been arrested,
And charged for driving my car.

I much prefer happy endings, don't you?

My son, Jeff, and his wife, Raelyn, sure do. They live on a farm surrounded by a thousand head of cattle, a team of horses, a flock of sheep, and a dozen piglets that sometimes get loose and squeal on each other.

As the first snowfall descended one year, Jeff and Raelyn decided to add two golden retrievers, Abby and Henry, to the mix. My wife and I shook our heads. Ah, the energy of youth.

Winter finally succumbed to spring, then staggered around again, unwelcome to all but children and rabid skiers. The landscape of green with its veins of brown lay a foot beneath the white stuff. Abby the retriever was pregnant and past due. She waddled through the drifts, grinning. But when the temperature plunged and the bitter winds blew, Jeff and Raelyn pulled her inside where she stood panting, her tongue at the exact height as the face of our very first grandchild, Sophia, the one who made me an Instagrampa.

To be pawed and licked by a dog this size is an experience you don't soon get over. But Sophie giggled and laughed like a seal that had just swallowed a sardine. And all was well.

Until someone left a door open, and Abby escaped.

Jeff and Raelyn looked in the cradle and under the table but nowhere could Abby be found. They scoured the yard. The field. The woods. At age two, Sophie did her best to pick up the scent. She wandered around, her hands upturned. "Abby, where you go? Come, Abby." But no Abby. About to give up, Sophie's parents told her that God loves all creatures great and small. And so the three of them prayed.

But winter wasn't going anywhere. That night, as darkness pressed down its thumb, the temperature dipped to -5°. The wind howled. Papa Henry howled. Still no Abby. The family prayed again. So did we. But the dog had been missing for two days.

And then, on the morning of the third day, Henry ran up to Raelyn, caught her sleeve in his teeth, coaxed her to the door, and took off running. Raelyn grabbed a coat and followed. She found Henry standing by an old tree stump, wagging his tail like proud papa dogs do in the movies. Beneath that stump was a small hole in the ground. From that hole came the unmistakable sound of whimpering.

Jeff arrived then. He pulled a very cold Abby from that tight little den. Rushed the dog inside to warm her up. Then reached his arm down that hole and began pulling out puppies. He brought them into the house two at a time. Sophie squealed. Raelyn warmed them. Two puppies. Four puppies. Six puppies. Very cold puppies. Jeff gently plunked the final five into a gaping bucket and showed them to his very wide-eyed wife. Eleven puppies. All warm and whining and looking for Mama.

Ever since I was a child, I have loved few things more than a story of the lost being found. Maybe the seeds were sown with that nursery rhyme about a poor little kitty. Or maybe there's a longing within each of us to know that someone found us worth looking for. That we are loved unreasonably. That someone called our name and didn't stop searching until we were back in the kennel.

Jesus told stories of lost sheep and lost coins and lost boys. He said he came "to seek and to save that which was lost" (Luke 19:10 NKJV).

I'm so glad.

Surely step 1 on the pathway to peace is finding a love greater than our own. A love from which nothing in all creation can separate us.

This weekend, I will visit Sophia. And we will stand beside that tree stump along with two or three or eleven puppies. We'll point and laugh. And have our faces licked. And later, I'll rock Sophia to sleep while telling her the story of how Jesus found me.

Then perhaps I'll sing her a nursery rhyme—with a happy ending.

Eleven puppies and a little lamb: Sophia Ramona Lynn Callaway, age 2.

3

Nine Minutes to Live

 Can you believe how many people are forecasting the end of the world? I mean, they're making predictions like there's no tomorrow.

If God be our God, He will give us peace in trouble. When there is a storm without, He will make peace within. The world can create trouble in peace, but God can create peace in trouble.

THOMAS WATSON

Few spots on earth are as desirable for a Canadian as Hawaii in January. But if you go, the key to keeping your friendships intact is to slip away without anyone knowing.

And so it is that Ramona and I find ourselves on a pristine beach one sunny Saturday, while comrades back home try to stop their teeth from chattering. My friend James tracks us down by phone. I tell him we aren't enjoying ourselves at all. The sun is too bright. We had to buy sunglasses. The sand in my shorts itches. Besides, I have to speak tomorrow. We're here suffering for Jesus.

"Cry me a river," he says, then hangs up.

It isn't the last I'll see of my phone today.

Back in our room, we are enjoying a lazy breakfast when suddenly the world goes crazier than a cageful of monkeys. At precisely 8:07 a.m., a zillion cell phones buzz, and a message flashes onscreen:

> *Ballistic missile threat inbound to Hawaii. Seek immediate shelter. This is not a drill.*

Now, I'd be a liar if I told you my first thought is, *Woohoo! Bring it on!* I have a family. Lots of air miles I haven't used. And where is this shelter? Beneath a palm tree?

Below our hotel room, pandemonium breaks loose. People panic. Some scream and flee through the streets.

"It's North Korea," someone yells. "It takes a ballistic missile twenty minutes to get here." Eleven minutes have come and gone.

With nine minutes to live, Ramona and I descend nine flights of stairs. I'm a little wobbly, dazed, fearful. A lady is carrying a Bible. "That's a good book," I say.

She laughs. "The best. Especially this morning." She holds up her phone. Call us delusional, but we stop and talk about heaven, about the hope we've found because of God's love.

"We're in good hands," she says. We all agree. And we hug a complete stranger like we're old friends.

With six minutes of our lives left, Ramona and I turn west onto Lewers Street toward the Pacific. The colors around us seem brighter now that the end is nigh, as if the sun has strewn its dazzling offspring all over the island.

A hundred thoughts flood your mind when you have five minutes to live. *The kids. Is there anything unsaid? No. They know we love them. Know where our new address will be. Know where the will is. All $62 of it.*

"I wonder if we'll see the missile," I say. "Let's watch."

Four minutes to live, and I'm thinking about the North Korean dictator. I haven't met him. Don't know if he can hit a basketball hoop from five feet, let alone pinpoint this tiny island 5,000 miles away. But stranger things have happened. "Help!" we pray.

Three minutes left to live, and a man stops us. He's furious at politicians. "We can't put our hope there," I say. "Our hope is in God." I kind of like the new me. I'm braver than normal. What's he going to do? Kill me?

With two minutes left, I realize it's important to know that my worldview works. I'm happy to report that Christianity does. I'm a little jittery, but there's a peace I can't explain. But for many others, fear reigns. One lifts a manhole cover and pushes a child below. Tearful goodbyes are said. Underground parking lots are filled. "There's no place to hide," someone says. "No refuge."

And something clicks. A verse learned in childhood.

I hold my wife's hand and tell her, "God is our refuge and strength, an ever-present help in trouble. Therefore we will not fear, though the earth give way and the mountains fall into the heart of the sea."[1]

One minute to live, and we are laughing. There are the mountains. There's the sea. There's not much else around here.

My watch says time's up.

I pause.

"We're still here," I say.

"Shoot," says Ramona.

We are laughing again. Most of her family is in heaven now. There are days she'd love to join them. Today isn't that day.

It takes a whopping 38 minutes for authorities to issue a retraction. Someone hit the wrong button. Oops. How prominent *is* this button? Did they hire a bit of a joker? What if his eyesight wasn't up to par? Maybe he pushed the button thinking it said, "Go for lunch," when it said, "Go for launch."

It's too early to "go for launch," so we continue our walk along Waikiki Beach. It's the emptiest we've seen it, but people are beginning to return.[2] I want to yell, "Don't go back to the way you were. Are you ready to go? You have one life to live. One story to tell. Write it well."

Half an hour ago this beach was crammed with people who are told how to look young, eat right, be healthy, stay buff. We cling to this planet for dear life, forgetting that our life here just might end a whole lot sooner than we think. Life is transitory. Those who make the most of it have faced the fact that this is not the land of the living—it's the land of the dying.

Perhaps we all need a missile scare once in a while. We'd be a little more aware that we're not here long. A little more prepared to make today count. To live for something that will outlast us.

At 10:00 a.m., another message flashes on my device: *You okay?* My friend James has been watching the news.

Yep, I reply. *But believe me, it's been a blast.*

4

The Fear-Driven Life

 I have a fear of speed bumps. But I'm getting over it.

The presence of anxiety is unavoidable,
but the prison of anxiety is optional.

MAX LUCADO

Lest you think from reading my missile-to-paradise story that I get up each morning, don my "No Fear" hat, and stride bravely into the world quoting comforting Bible verses, it's not so. Since I was about ten, anxiety has greeted me at some point each day.

I could blame my mother's panic attacks or the bullies who found me a desirable target (I had the lethal combination of a big mouth and a small body), but fear and anxiety visit us all.

Back in the last century, the government in its finite wisdom instituted a drill called "Duck and Cover." Our teacher interrupted math class and commanded us to lunge beneath our desks and place our hands over our tiny heads. This terrified most of the children. Not me. School was unbearably boring; this was the highlight of my day.

I had no idea that world leaders were experiencing itchy trigger fingers around nuclear weaponry, so some bureaucrat had the bright idea that children would be safest beneath wooden desks. Yes, this would be the key to survival in the event of an atomic attack. One day we would tell our grandchildren, "Atom bombs exploded. But we were fine. Others weren't. But we had very solid desks, and we hid beneath them."

During one such "Duck and Cover," a classmate started blubbering, then told me exactly why we were under there: "Someone wants us dead." And anxiety began to take up residence.

Fear says, "Duck!" Anxiety says, "Duck, and think about it a while. I mean, *what if*?"

By 1955, more than 20 percent of Americans thought humans would disappear from the planet by 1960.[1] That didn't stop them from building houses, acquiring mortgages, and investing in pension plans, but many thought the end was nigh. By the 1970s, books like *The Late Great Planet Earth* were flying off store shelves, and when the year 2000 arrived despite the Y2K scare, my parents agreed with obvious disappointment, "We never thought we'd see the year 2000."

Today, anxiety has reached epidemic proportions. The big hand on the Doomsday Clock sits at 11:58, the closest it's been to midnight since 1953.[2] I like telling audiences that my biggest fear is having a heart attack while playing the game charades. Imagine. You're clutching your chest—*and they're guessing*. Yes, I have been hamstrung by anxiety. It's like I'm back in second grade, hands over my head, allowing anxiety to steal my peace.

Fear can be a healthy thing, of course. For some, fear of jail is the beginning of wisdom. Fear of lung cancer helped a friend of mine kick a pack-a-day habit. Fear of licking metal doorknobs in winter kept my tongue intact (except for that fateful day in 1965). But anxiety over circumstances we can't control defeats us in a thousand ways—choking our courage, stealing our joy.

An acquaintance of mine has taken to forwarding every frightening video he can lay his mouse on. Evil is spreading. Everything is wrong. I phoned him after watching one. "I got your video," I said.

"What do you think? Freaky, huh?"

"I think God must be very, very worried," I said.

There was a pause. "Uh…you're joking, right?"

I was. We live in dark times. But God does amazing work in the dark.

Anxiety is a no-confidence vote in God. It pulverizes our effectiveness and paralyzes our joy. Change begins as we embrace the next five sentences. Read them slowly.

> Don't fret or worry. Instead of worrying, pray. Let petitions and praises shape your worries into prayers, letting God know your concerns. Before you know it, a sense of God's wholeness, everything coming together for good, will come and settle you down. It's wonderful what happens when Christ displaces worry at the center of your life (Philippians 4:6-7 MSG).

When I was a kid, my parents taught me to pray, "If I should die before I wake…" I thought, *What am I gonna die of? I'm four. Hardening of the arteries? Kidney stones? Osteoporosis?* And then my older brother threatened to kill me, and my prayers took on new urgency.

I'm still in second grade at the School of Prayer. But I've noticed that when anxiety arrives, those who place Jesus at the center of their lives instinctively shoo it out through the door of prayer. The more we pray, the less we panic.

One week after Nelson and Linda Reed faced their greatest fear head on, Linda wrote these words to me: "God is so good, and all his ways are good—yes, even in this! God is taking me through my deepest fear—the sudden, violent death of my child one day before his thirtieth birthday. But we are seeing God's sweetness in all the details. Christ is walking with me through it. He did not leave me to go it alone. He is exchanging my fear for acceptance, peace, even joy!"

Christ had displaced anxiety at the center of Linda's life.

What lies at the very core of your life?
Money? What if you lose it?
Family? What if they disappoint?
Beauty? What if it fades?
Career? What if it ends?
Or is it Christ?
What we place at the center will feed fear or feed faith.

None of us knows what lies ahead, but God does. And he has promised to walk with us through it, to give enough light for the next step.

And though it's hard to see him sometimes, nothing can separate us from God's love. He is in the middle of whatever has happened, is happening, and will happen to us. So let's crawl out from beneath our wooden desks and look to him—before we have a heart attack.

5

Water Has Broken

 Have you heard of this new trend of giving birth in a pool? They say it's less traumatic for the baby. But, it's gotta be pretty traumatic for the other people in the pool.

The old system of having a baby was much better than the new system, the old system being characterized by the fact that the man didn't have to watch.

DAVE BARRY

How very little can be done under the spirit of fear.

FLORENCE NIGHTINGALE

One Saturday two phone calls arrived in rapid succession. The first was from my son Steve. "Dad, my water heater broke. It's leaking all over the place. What do I do? Help!" I have no idea why he would call a guy like me. Comfort and condolences I can offer. Mechanical abilities? Not so much. I am remotely aware of the fact that hot showers contain hot water, but I have no idea how water gets hot or where it comes from. The basement, I think.

"Shut off the taps," I advised. "Mop up. Call your uncle Bill. He's a plumber."

I pushed the off button, and the phone buzzed again. It was my daughter Rachael. "Daddy," she said, "my water broke." On April 1 she had said the same thing; this time I knew it was no joke. The contractions were 15 minutes apart, I think she said, which sounded urgent to me. Twenty-four hours of labor had begun.

Times have changed through the years in the Having Children department. When I was born, my father was 2,000 miles away in Miami, Florida, on business. That's how it was back then. Dads were not allowed in the same area code as their wives during childbirth. No one knows exactly why, but it may have something to do with the fact that guys were known for fainting in the delivery room. "Look, Bob! That's the placenta!" *Wham.* Then everyone had to keep stepping over Bob.

Some cutting-edge hospitals were particularly accommodating, allowing expectant fathers to sit in the waiting room as long as they kept quiet and didn't faint. But most dads stood outside the building, much like smokers do now. If they were seized by an urge to smoke, they could find a smoking room in the hospital. The surgeon general might be in there chatting with doctors about the health benefits of first- and secondhand smoke.

Not anymore. Months before my daughter's water broke, she sent out formal requests inviting her husband, mother, best friend, and doula, which I had not heard of until recently, to the delivery room. Apparently a doula is someone who has had at least nine children herself, so she is qualified to offer practical assistance and emotional support when the screaming begins. Plus, she brings crackers and cheese to the birthing room while her husband stays home with the kids—which is what I was doing.

I was babysitting granddaughter Sophia—unaided, I might add—when my wife called to tell me that the doula was running out of food and needed more snacks, mostly lactose-free cheese and organic fruit. Would I bring them? Of course I would. I bundled up Sophie and strapped her into a 200-pound car seat.

And suddenly, there I was. Standing in my own daughter's

delivery room. My dad would have been shocked and maybe even impressed. Worship music was playing. The doula was taking pictures. I offered words of comfort to my daughter. "Rachael, keep telling yourself this: Most people throughout history have been born this way. It's gonna be okay. I can do this." Then I hugged her. And fainted. Not really. But I did leave with great haste.

Back home, as I held little Sophie, I remembered another phone call from my daughter 12 months earlier. "Daddy," she said, "we lost the baby." In the midst of darkness and uncertainty, God had heard our prayers for another child. Another miracle. Still, anxiety troubled me. Into what kind of a world are we bringing these children?

My wife's well-worn Bible was eight inches from my elbow. I flipped it open to Psalm 78. Highlighted in neon yellow were these words: "We will tell the next generation about the glorious deeds of the LORD…his power and his mighty wonders…He commanded our ancestors to teach them to their children, so the next generation might know them…and they in turn will teach their own children. So each generation should set its hope anew on God, not forgetting his glorious miracles and obeying his commands."[1]

"Times are dark," I whispered to Sophie. "But you're in good hands."

Early Sunday morning we welcomed our second cute-beyond-words grandbaby. I was lovestruck. Despite my suggestion that they name her Phyllis in my honor, she is named after the courageous *Lord of the Rings* character Éowyn.

Welcome to our world, Eowyn.

Jesus is here. And I'm here too.

You're going to like me a lot.

I'm going to feed you ice cream before your parents want me to. Then we'll all go over to your uncle's place, where you can have a nice warm bath. After all, he has himself a brand-new water heater.

6

Wrong Number?

 Nothing brings people together nowadays quite like a broken elevator.

Those who have not yet seen a miracle need to open their eyes and go looking. I live on the Canadian prairies. One happens each spring.

JAMES ENNS

Some people are not just funny, they're surprisingly quick. Mary Chambers draws hilarious cartoons for magazines the world over. When I first phoned her to see if she would draw some for me, I thought I had the wrong number. In my defense, Mary sounds even younger than she is. This is an actual transcript of our conversation:

> Me: "Hello, um, is your mother there?"
>
> Mary: "No. My husband won't let her live here."
>
> Me: "Ha ha ha ha ha…I think I'm gonna—"
>
> Mary: "Are you okay?"

Nearly 90 percent of humans over six years of age now own a phone, which leads to some hilarious wrong number stories.

Another Mary was looking for a guy named Michael, but mistakenly called a guy named Roger. Roger didn't know a Michael. But Mary wouldn't quit. She called often. Thankfully, Roger had a good sense of humor.

> Roger: "Hello?"
>
> Mary: "Michael, is that you?"
>
> Roger: "No Mary, you got the wrong number again."
>
> Mary: "Michael?"
>
> Roger: "Michael's not here, Mary."
>
> Mary: "Oh, okay. Have him call me when he gets home."

Right before the 9/11 attacks, Reg got a call from a guy who was looking for a restaurant in Los Angeles. "I told him he had the wrong area code," said Reg. "This was an apartment in DC. He laughed and asked how the weather was. I told him, and we had a short chat. The morning of 9/11 I got a call from the same guy; he wanted to make sure I was okay."

My favorite wrong number story comes from Sajanth. Born in Sri Lanka, he immigrated with his family to Canada when he was six. They were practicing Hindus. "We went to temple every Tuesday and Friday," Sajanth remembers. "We regularly gave offerings and prayed to the hundreds of gods whose statues and photos dotted our apartment."

But all was not well. Sajanth's father abused alcohol—and his family. Sajanth was just 16 when his dad left home for good. His mother did what she could, but the pressure of raising three children alone in a rough Toronto neighborhood was overwhelming. At wits' end, she decided to consult a Hindu astrologer.

Picking up the phone, she dialed the number she'd been given. A woman answered, "Hello?"

"Are you the astrologer?"

"No, I'm afraid you have the wrong number."

Sajanth's mother was shocked. The woman had answered in Tamil, her native tongue.

"Why do you want an astrologer?"

"I…uh…want to know what my family's future is going to be like."

The woman paused. "I know someone who can do that," she said. "He has our future in his hands."

Sajanth's mother listened as the lady told her of God's great love for her. That he sent his Son, Jesus. That he didn't come to earth to condemn it, but to love and save it. All she had to do was believe in Jesus, and she wouldn't perish but have everlasting life. "It is by grace we are saved, through faith," she said, "It's not because of the good works we do. It's a gift from God."[1]

They talked a while longer, then the woman asked, "Would you and your family like to go to church with me?"

Sajanth will never forget that day. The music. The story of a Savior who loved him. His decision to follow Jesus. And over time, his mother and the rest of his family joined him.

He smiles whenever he thinks of that phone call. "When you consider the thousands of possibilities in a seven-digit phone number, the odds of my mother dialing a number that would go to a Bible-believing Tamil speaker are almost impossible to compute."

"I guess God had a plan for me," says Sajanth, still smiling. "I never really knew who I was until I discovered who he is."

And who is he?

Sajanth knows him as the creator and sustainer of all things. As his redeemer. He is holy and just. He is love. He is not willing that any should perish. That is just the start.

And who are we? In tenth grade an exasperated teacher crossed his arms and said, "Callaway, just who do you think you are?" My answer was not worth repeating. It has changed radically through the years.

I am…

- created in God's image (Genesis 1:26)

- dearly loved (Romans 5:8)

- redeemed and forgiven by God's grace (Colossians 1:14)

- adopted by God (Ephesians 1:5)

- free from condemnation (Romans 8:1)

- called to bear good fruit (John 15:16)

- heir to a fortune that is out of this world (Romans 8:17)

Lasting joy is elusive until we understand who we are and *whose* we are. Just ask Sajanth. He'll tell you that when God has you on speed dial, he also has a purpose for your life. Today Sajanth pastors a church in Toronto, Ontario. He has a family who loves Jesus. And not long before I completed this story, Sajanth's father put his faith in Jesus too.

It all began with a "wrong" number.

7

Cheer Me Up

 A new study is out. Women who are just a little bit overweight live longer…than the men who point it out to them.

Joy is the settled assurance that God is in control of all the details of my life, the quiet confidence that ultimately everything is going to be all right, and the determined choice to praise God in all things.

KAY WARREN

One evening before I took to the stage, a lady came up to me and said, "I've had a hard day. You better be funny."

I said, "Honey, that's not fair."

True story. It was my wife.

We all need cheering up, don't we?

I love the story of a small boy who picked up the phone when it rang. "Hello?"

"May I speak to your parents?" a voice said.

"They're busy," the boy whispered.

"Oh. Is anybody else there?"

"Yes. The police."

"May I speak to one of the police officers, please?"

"They're busy."

"Oh. Well, is anyone else there?"

"Yes. The firemen."

"May I speak to one of the firemen then?"

"They're busy."

"So let me get this straight—your parents, the police, and the firemen are there, but they're all busy? What are they doing?"

"They're looking for me."

I wonder how long that guy laughed after hanging up. Maybe he needed a good laugh. If you do, too, consider this your phone call.

Years ago I first encountered church bulletin bloopers. Boy, did I laugh. Thankfully, they're still making church bulletins. And they're still making bloopers. Here are a few favorites:

- "Congratulations to Tim and Rhonda on the birth of their daughter October 12 through 17."

- "If you choose to heave during the postlude, please do so quietly."

- "The Advent Retreat will be held in the lover level of St. Mary's Cathedral."

- "As soon as the weather clears up, the men will have a goof outing."

- "We pray that our people will jumble themselves."

- "Bertha Belch, a missionary from Africa, will be speaking tonight. Come hear Bertha Belch all the way from Africa."

- "This evening's sermon topic will be 'What is Hell?' Come early and listen to our choir practice."

- "Women's Luncheon: Each member bring a sandwich. Polly Phillips will give the medication."

Laughter is great medication. Especially when joy is hard to find and our lives read like a blooper reel. One of my friends likes to say, "Life is hard, and then you die." Well, life *is* hard sometimes, but whatever you face, keep in mind these three biblical reminders of why we can rejoice.

1. **Undying love.** "Because of the LORD's great love we are not consumed, for his compassions never fail. They are new every morning; great is your faithfulness" (Lamentations 3:22-23 NIV). "His unfailing love toward those who fear him is as great as the height of the heavens above the earth" (Psalm 103:11).

2. **Unending companionship.** "Be strong and courageous. Do not be afraid; do not be discouraged, for the LORD your God will be with you wherever you go" (Joshua 1:9 NIV).

3. **Unseen rewards.** "Our present troubles are small and won't last very long. Yet they produce for us a glory that vastly outweighs them and will last forever! So we don't look at the troubles we can see now; rather, we fix our gaze on things that cannot be seen. For the things we see now will soon be gone, but the things we cannot see will last forever" (2 Corinthians 4:17-18).

I had the pleasure of golfing with Max Lucado. He told me of a 78-year-old friend he golfed with. Like most of us, Max's friend had exciting plans for retirement—until his wife began her battle with Parkinson's. Medication and struggle became the norm. Her needs became his constant concern. Yet he never complained. In fact, he was often ready with a smile or joke.

His secret? Each morning, Max's friend and his wife sat together and sang the old hymn, "Count Your Blessings" by Johnson Oatman Jr. And they did just that. Listed off the truth of their many, many blessings. Jerry said, "That does much more to relieve her pain and my anxiety than any of her meds could do."

When Ramona's grand mal seizures were taking hold of her each day, I grew increasingly bitter. But deep in my soul, a change began to awaken the day I lay beside her on the floor doing what I could to protect her while she thrashed about. Suddenly, I thought to myself, *I was here to catch her this time. She wasn't alone. Thank you, God.*

He began in me a work that has been slow going. But step-by-step he is relieving me of amnesia when it comes to my abundant blessings.

In the midst of it all, I found no other faith that could sustain me. No other worldview where suffering is seen as a meaningful part of life. Christianity never denies the sorrow of it. Never explains the fairness of it. But it does provide purpose in it. I have seen suffering deliver to my door more compassion for others; I have seen it drive me deeper into God's love than I ever imagined.

The single greatest act we can engage in if our life is to be stamped by joy is to go looking for blessings. And when we find them, we tell others: our neighbors, the guy on the phone. Maybe the police and firemen too.

8

Big Hairy Deal

 I give thanks for small mercies. Like the fact that my hair is still growing—even if it's mostly coming out my ears.

Those complain first...who have the least to do. The gift of grumbling is largely dispensed among those who have no other talents, or who keep what they have wrapped up in a napkin.

CHARLES SPURGEON

found myself complaining today. "My electric toothbrush died," I told my wife. "Now I have to move my arm."

She massaged my sore arm and said, "Aw. Life is hard." So I grumbled about that too.

Few would disagree that we have become a culture of complaint. Here are actual grievances launched by disgruntled humans:

"My hand is too chubby to shove into the Pringle's Chip container, so I have to tilt the container."

"I went into the bathroom with my socks on and the floor was wet and now my socks are wet."

"My phone is too fat for my skinny jeans."

"My husband does everything I ask him to do, but why do I have to ask him?"

Our daughter worked as a waitress, so she knows a little about complaints. She was instructed to ask, "Is everything okay?" and sometimes felt like asking, "Is *anything* okay?" Here are some protests muttered in eateries:

- "I'm sending the fish back. It was staring at me."
- "The plate color clashes with my food. It's too ugly to Instagram."
- "This cup is right-handed. I'm left-handed."
- "My seedless watermelon has a seed in it."
- "I'm sending the chicken back. I ordered it medium rare."

The best customer complaint of all time was tweeted to Domino's: "Yoooo, I ordered a pizza and [it] came with no toppings on it or anything, it's just bread."[1] Domino's responded that they were sorry and asked the complainant to indicate where it happened so they could set things right. Not much later, the customer tweeted again: "Never mind, I opened the pizza upside down."[2]

When our friend Liz graduated from nursing school, we took her and her husband, Gord, to a fine restaurant to celebrate. I ordered lime chicken smothered in mushrooms and hemmed in by veggies. The waitress brought the food and stood by graciously waiting as we uttered a quick prayer of thanks for the meal and the occasion.

Minutes later, she returned to ask how everything was.

"Fantastic," I said.

And then, as she walked away, I bit into the chicken.

Now, it occurs to me that you may be reading this while eating dinner, so I shall attempt, as delicately as possible, to tell you what ensued.

Did you ever pop something into your mouth and suddenly realize it was not what you expected? Well, nowhere had the menu listed,

"Lime chicken stuffed with an 18-inch hair." You may say, "Big hairy deal." But trust me, it is most difficult to remove a hair of this span with dignity and grace. I tried. But the hair kept coming. My wife raised a hand to her mouth and gasped. I raised a cloth napkin to my mouth and gagged. The eyes of my friends were the size of their dinner plates.

And then Ramona started to laugh.

Without that laugh, this could have been a very hairy situation.

"It was the look on your face," she said. "I couldn't help it." Such is her sense of humor—finding hilarity in my discomfort.

"I'm gonna throw this thing over my shoulder and show the kitchen staff," I said.

The waitress heard the laughter and came to check on us. "Um, don't tell anyone just yet," I said, "but there's a hair in my chicken."

She gasped. "It's not one of mine, is it?"

"No. It's far longer than yours." I pointed to where it was peeking out from under a napkin. She gasped some more. "It's not one of mine, is it?" I asked, patting my bald head. She laughed. Then gasped again. She couldn't stop apologizing. I told her we were okay. We visit third-world countries where you don't want to know what's in the chicken. "The rest of the food is very good," I said.

She was visibly relieved. "Would you like dessert?" she asked.

My friend Gord loves puns. He said we'd *mullet* over.

Now, of course there's a time to point out what's wrong. But I think we followers of Jesus should be known for our grace and gratitude, for treating well those who serve us. After all, the ultimate servant has called us to serve. And I sometimes wonder what would happen if we were known for overtipping.

Over ice cream sundaes at a different restaurant, we couldn't stop laughing about the Great Hair Incident and all we can be grateful for when encountering such things in one's chicken. After all, 1 Thessalonians 5:18 doesn't say, "In good things give thanks." It says, "In *every*thing give thanks" (NKJV, emphasis added).

Joy grows best in the soil of thanksgiving.

So Ramona got us started. "The hair had been cooked."

Liz added, "You had a nurse nearby in case you choked."

I was thankful I wasn't charged extra for the hair. And I got a free meal.

Gord said, "The restaurant had *hair* conditioning."

"Aw Gord, enough with the puns."

"Rest *a-sheared*," he replied, "I have more hair puns, but I'll *shave* them for later."

9

Magnetic Personality

 When I was a kid, my mom made sure I was part of social networking. She said, "Go outside and play."

Human beings, being what they are, somehow feel entitled to question the reasons for everything that happens to them...We are often quick to forget our blessings, slow to forget our misfortunes.

W. PHILLIP KELLER

A girl took her hamster to the vet. It hadn't moved in three days. Wouldn't eat. Wouldn't drink. Just leaned up against the side of its cage. Stuck. The worried owner explained that the poor hamster had escaped before she found it under the fridge.

Frowning, the vets lifted the hamster from the cage. The critter began walking around the table as if all was well. They were baffled. Then they noticed a bulge in the hamster's cheek.

They pulled out a fridge magnet. *A fridge magnet.* While enjoying its freedom, the hamster had downed the magnet, then spent the next three days stuck to the side of its cage, thanks to its "magnetic personality."[1]

I'm like that hamster. Maybe you are too. Circumstances have us paralyzed: That job loss. That phone call. That uncertain market. That relationship. We all love to laugh, but at times we're stuck to the side of our cage.

When I was a kid, I looked around our church and thought, *Some of these people are cranky.* Ever met a cranky Christian? Ever *been* one? When I was informed that I would spend eternity with these people, I was less than ecstatic. To me, "joyful Christian" was an oxymoron. Like airline food or jumbo shrimp.

My exasperated fifth-grade teacher in our Christian school told me, "There's a bus leaving in ten minutes. Be under it." A Sunday School teacher, after an hour with 12 of us fourth-grade boys looked so sour he could suck buttons off a sofa. In hindsight, I don't blame him. But these are occupations for which you do not enlist without a good sense of humor.

Recently, a guy said to me, "I don't laugh outwardly, but I'm really quite joyful inside. This is just the face God gave me."

I smiled and said, "Tell your face about your joy. A stifled laugh is gonna back up on you and spread to your hips. So let it go."

Sadly, some of us haven't made the good news look so good. But it is. We have been forgiven. Eternity is waiting. Nothing in all of history tops this good news. Nothing in all the world can steal it. The most important issues were dealt with by our Savior, Jesus, on the cross, and we're free to rejoice. This should spread across our conversations, our relationships, and our faces too.

When the great preacher Jonathan Edwards was just 18, he delivered what was likely his first sermon.[2] It was on Christian happiness. He had three main points, summarized well by Justin Buzzard.[3]

1. **"Our bad things will turn out for good."** Romans 8:28 says, "We know that in all things God works for the good of those who love him, who have been called according to his purpose" (NIV). We are promised that bad things will happen. Yet God

is performing miracles in the messes on this fallen planet. He is even doing this among annoying fourth and fifth grade boys. God is a redemptive God. He is at work in the seemingly impossible.

2. **"Our good things can never be taken."** When my brother-in-law Bill was nursing his wife through the final stages of Huntington's, these were life-giving words. Whatever came, he was assured of God's presence, God's purpose, and God's peace. He knew that the truly good things were the permanent things.

3. **"The best things are yet to come."** As believers, we cling tenaciously to the truth that love has the final move. That nothing, no matter how mysterious or painful, can ever separate us from God's love. A friend smiles whenever someone says, "It's all good." He has walked through too many valleys to say this. But sometimes he tells himself, "Everything will be alright in the end. If it's not alright, it's not the end."

Like that hamster, we're tempted to swallow the wrong stuff. I think it's time we fixed our thoughts on things that are true, honorable, right, pure, lovely, admirable. Things that are excellent and worthy of praise.[4]

Maybe it's time we put those words on a fridge magnet. Just keep it away from your hamster.

10

Forbidden Smile

 I'm a grandpa, and I love it. But the night I became a grandpa, I sat straight up in bed at about three in the morning and thought, *I'm sleeping with a grandma.* Sorry, but it just seemed a little weird at the time.

The major mark of justified believers is joy.
JOHN STOTT

Freaking out has become wildly popular. Everyone's doing it. Some enjoy it—like those who bring you the nightly news. Their jobs depend on it. The anchor bids you a good evening, then spends an entire hour telling you why it isn't.[1]

Pick up a parenting book. Chances are you'll also pick up a boatload of anxiety. *Your child should sleep on her back. No, wait—her front. No, wait—her back.* Search the web. *You're not paying enough for your child's education. If he fails, you are to blame. If he succeeds, well, that won't happen. You've been slipping him sugar since he was six, haven't you?*

Read the latest study. *Coffee will help you live long and prosper.* No, wait—that was last week. This week I read that coffee raises your risk of heart disease. Hold that latte. And dark chocolate? It may be good for you, but be warned: consuming large amounts can lead to an increased heart rate, diarrhea, irritability, anxiety, and gas.

Sometimes it takes a little child to remind us to step back and relax a little.

There are seven wonders of the world, I'm told. But for a child, there are a thousand. We were in a mall surrounded by frenzied shoppers, and my granddaughter Eowyn couldn't get over how many people there were. She had to say hi to everyone. And bye too. Shoppers were laughing. She pointed up at a mannequin and said, "Bumpa." Which is me. I'm Bumpa. I saw no resemblance at all. Except that the mannequin was completely bald.

She likes to smile and point: "Car! Plane! Car! Plane!" I think she wants to get away from us. If she says, "Passport," lock the doors; we're in trouble.

Her cousin Claira was eight months old when my son Jeff and his wife, Raelyn, took her to get her passport photo. Now, when I was a kid, you didn't need a passport. No one had much for identification back then. Complete strangers showed up at family reunions, and you had no way of verifying who they were. But if a baby can't prove who she is these days, she can't go far. So Claira arrived all groomed and proper. To the photographer's horror, he realized immediately that he had a nightmare on his hands. No, she didn't scream. She didn't have a tantrum. It was worse.

She wouldn't stop smiling.

And in the world of passport photos, this is a cardinal sin.

To make matters worse, Claira was like a small Pentecostal octopus, constantly throwing her arms in the air. So Jeff held down her tentacles as the poor guy snapped away, shaking his head as she smiled at the wall. The camera. A light stand. "Not good," he kept saying. But Claira wouldn't stop. The photos were coming out far too sweet. It was a disaster. The weary photographer looked around for something—anything—to make her stop. No lemons or prunes could be found, so he dabbed her tongue with tissue paper. "This might work," he said. It didn't. The girl was incorrigible.

"Stop smiling, Claira." But an eight-month-old doesn't understand. She smiled at the carpet, the lights, an ashtray. It was like she believed that a smile is the prettiest thing you can wear. It was a catastrophe.

At last, the photographer chose the least smiley photo. "You can try it. But I'm sure I'll see you back here in an hour," he said.

The passport officer squinted at it and frowned, then issued a minor warning. "She's smiling," he said. But wonder of wonders, he gave his stamp of approval. By the time Claira's next passport picture is taken, she will know better.

If this girl could talk, I wonder what she'd say. Perhaps she's so fresh from heaven, she just can't stop smiling. Maybe she'd say, "You people need to lighten up. I mean, what's the big deal? You should see what things are like where I just came from. God holds it all in his hands. It's gonna be okay. So smile."

She will discover soon enough that the world around us steals our smile every day. Bad news. Stress. Headaches and heartaches. Bills, ills, wills, and not nearly enough thrills. But for now she says, "Why so serious? Do this." Claira agrees with Phyllis Diller: "A smile is a curve that sets everything straight."

Years ago in London, England, an old man stopped a lady at a train station. "Excuse me, ma'am," he said, "I want to thank you for something."

"Thank me?" the lady asked.

"Yes. I used to be a ticket collector here. Whenever you went by, you always gave me a cheerful smile and a 'Good morning.' You don't know what a difference it made to me. Rain or shine, it was always the same, and I said to myself, 'I wonder where she gets her smile from. One cannot always be happy, yet she seems to be.'

And I knew that smile must come from inside somehow. Then one morning you came by, and you had a little Bible in your hand. I said to myself, 'Perhaps that's where she got her smile from.' So as I went home that night I bought a Bible, and I've been reading it. I've found Jesus, and now I can smile too. I just want to thank you."

There are a dozen reasons to frown today. And a thousand reasons to smile. To rejoice. To break out in a contagious grin. Start here: *I'm alive. Fed. Clothed. Loved by God.*

Don't stop, little girl. Throw those octopus hands in the air and smile.

As for the rest of us, if you've forgotten where your smile is, don't worry. It's right there beneath your nose.

11

Mamma Mia!

 Last weekend our friends Liz and Gord were at a family gathering. Their three-year-old nephew was working on an ice cream cone. His mom said to him, "May I have a lick?" He gave her the strangest look. Then he took two steps toward her…and licked her arm.

We will parent imperfectly, our children will make their own choices, and God will mysteriously and wondrously use it all to advance his kingdom.

LESLIE FIELDS

My daughter Rachael is a mother of three who loves her kids but suffers from debilitating exhaustion. She's not alone.

Today's mother must ensure that her child's physical, emotional, social, academic, intellectual, environmental, and nutritional needs are met while he remains in his car seat until he's five foot eleven.

Today's mother must feed her 1.3 children a diet fortified by sugar-free, gluten-free, dairy-free, peanut-free, calorie-free, pesticide-free, free-range, hand-shucked lettuce leaves. When I was a child, we chewed gum off the sidewalk.

Today's mother must know how to post creative baby announcements on Pinterest and Instagram. She must host woodland-themed baby showers complete with deer antlers and bunny-shaped macarons. And get her body back after birth. She must be primed at any moment to speak with acumen on the pros and cons of formula, onesies, vaccinations, and the many uses of coconut oil.

Today's mother must hold her child close, foster independence, and know how to blend pure essential oils. She must keep her child processed foods–free, plastic-free, and screen-free. She must know when to Google "my baby has a cold," then resist panic when the results advise her to contact the head of pediatrics for the World Health Organization immediately because the child could have a rare toxic disorder.

When I was a child, I was just glad if my mother could find the Vicks VapoRub.

Back then (and it wasn't so long ago) Mom left me outdoors for hours, where I ate dirt and bugs while she baked homemade chocolate chip cookies with genetically modified white sugar. I have no idea how we lived. We ate hot dogs straight off the floor one time because Mom said, "You kids will be fine. I washed the floors last September." Mothers could get away with those things back then. Not now.

Being a parent in any generation from time immemorial has been a time-consuming, hair-raising, sleep-depriving experience. If you doubt me, try starting your stove tomorrow morning with wood and flint, then launder your cloth diapers by beating them with a stick while fending off wolves. Yet I don't think any previous society would envy what young moms are up against today.

Never before has a generation so structured its families around child life. *If they fail, I'll be at fault. If they succeed, I'll be complete.*

And so, my darling daughter Rachael with a four-year-old, toddler, and newborn, here's some guilt-free advice from your ever-lovin' dad.

You will be tempted to compare. Don't.

Forget Instagram and Facebook and the mothers whose glossy profile pictures are Photoshop perfect, whose kids are fully dressed by lunchtime. Forget a spotless house, a perfect perm, a finished to-do list. Dare not to compare. Aim lower sometimes. And stop listening to older people who say, "You just wait. The next stage is worse." We're still trying to figure out a punishment that fits their crime.

Stop freaking out.

It's a myth that somewhere out there is a perfect parent. You've often told me that my mom was your hero. Did you know she wasn't a great cook? She rarely drove me anywhere unless a bone needed to be set. Mom lived several time zones from perfect. But she spent time with me when she was able, taught me the Bible, took me to church, cried with me, laughed with me, said "sorry" when she needed to, loved my dad, disciplined me when I needed it, loved Jesus, and prayed like crazy.

Other than that, she was pretty much unemployed.

You don't need my permission, but allow me to voice it: Being crazy busy is not an admirable trait. Relax. Take breaks from your kids. Enroll them in fewer activities. Methinks we have made parenting more complex than it should be. When we raised you, we were content to feed and clothe you—and keep your brothers away from dynamite. For Pete's sake, stop freaking out!

You can do this.

You are actively engaged in one of the most vital missions on earth. I know it's like running the Boston Marathon. Except that there's no audience cheering—just needy miniature people staring at your torso, screaming for food. Your muscles and nerves may throb, but you're up to this. You can nap in spurts. You can keep your sense of humor amid screaming, griping, and raging guilt that threaten to steal your joy. And one day, just maybe, you will not sleep like a baby, but like your husband, and you will climb on the scale and see your toes again.

Lean on God.

Talk to God. Confide in him. He loves you and smiles on you. Psalm 28:7 is a great verse for tired mamas: "The Lord is my strength and my shield; my heart trusts in him, and he helps me" (NIV). Your children are loved, prayed for, and in the hands of a God who loves us unreasonably, who is entirely trustworthy.

And, like every other mother, you have an accuser.[1] One who whispers lies in your ear, calling you "Failure." "You're not pretty enough," he snarls, "smart enough, rich enough, talented enough. You're a bad mom. A bad wife. Your tiny contribution to the kingdom is a joke." Just tell him where to go, then go to the God who tells you the truth. You're his precious child, his heir—loved, forgiven, redeemed. God never asks you to do what he won't equip you to do. You can do this, by his strength alone.

And remember, the world will grind to a halt within a generation if you go on strike. So hang in there. You are loving these babies and pointing them heavenward. Lighten up and laugh. It's going to be okay. You have yet to put little Aaron in the dishwasher and the dishes in the stroller.

You are awesome.

12

Three Words That Changed Me

 I'm an optimist. I dropped a bowl of Jell-O on the floor, looked down, and thought, *I just created a masterpiece. I'm going to art school.*

There are two types of speakers: those who
are nervous and those who are liars.

MARK TWAIN

s it possible to make someone smile with three words? I think so. How about, "Hot apple pie"? Or, "Come for supper"? Or, "Let's go eat"? It sounds like I have a bit of a thing for food. Perhaps I do.

Is it possible to tell a three-word joke? Let me try. The only ones I know are bad puns, so bear with me. Bakers knead dough. Gloves are handy. Twins are "womb"-mates. Drillers are boring. Smoking's a drag. Teachers have class. Fleas bug me. Tailors suit me.

Please forgive me. Perhaps the only thing tougher to find than a three-word joke is a three-word joke that's funny.

Some three-word combinations are tough to take: "You're outa shape." "You are wrong." "You are fired." "Told you so." "You look tired."

I much prefer hearing one of these: "You are hired." "You are fabulous." "I brought sandwiches." There's that food thing again.

Three-word sentences have made my heart soar through the years: "Class is canceled." "Marry you? Yes!" "Congratulations! A son!" "I forgive you." "Be right there."

A friend dropped by my office. "Your red car," he said, "I hit it." Then he grinned and spoke three beautiful words, "I'm just kidding."

Who doesn't love hearing, "Fifty percent discount"? "Three day weekend"? "Free doughnut samples"?

I love it when my wife says, "You look great." "You're the best." "Come kiss me." "I like you a lot." Wait. I got carried away. That was five words.

Motivators live on three-word phrases: Seize the day. Aspire to inspire. Make it happen. Prove them wrong. Dreams come true. Do your best. Don't hold back. Don't stop believing.

Twenty-six years ago, three words changed me.

I had just written my first book and soon found myself on airplanes and stages. Public speaking and flying became my top fears. Thankfully, no one asked me to speak while flying—one nightmare at a time is bad enough—but publicists began sending me tickets so I could visit TV studios and thrill audiences with the prospect of purchasing my books. I traveled alone, scared saliva-less, strapped in a metal tube built by the lowest bidder, headed places I hadn't been to meet people I hadn't met.

One memorable day on one such flight, I pulled out a greeting card I'd stuffed in my briefcase the night before. My mother had handed it to me. I knew it contained no money; she didn't have much of the stuff. But its contents were gold. Rising from a flowery background was a Bible verse: "Be strong and courageous. Do not be afraid; do not be discouraged, for the LORD your God will be with you wherever you go" (Joshua 1:9 NIV).

Below this, Mom had written words of her own: "Dear Son, Dad and I are praying for you. God has allowed you to be such a blessing. We're so thankful you get to do this. Love, Mom."

Three words popped out at me. Did you see them? Read it again and look. I honestly don't think I'd have had the joy of doing what I've been doing the last 25 years were it not for those three words, which began to permeate my thinking and reconfigure my attitude.

"You get to."

God has allowed me to do this. Thousands would love to.

I don't *have* to. I *get* to.

Life can be filled with feelings of "I have to" and "I need to." But I wonder what our days would look like if we embraced a new attitude each morning. If we woke up and said, "Thank you, God. I don't have to go work; I *get* to. I don't have to parent these crazy teens or change this ripe diaper or deal with this annoying client. I *get* to. I don't have to plumb this sink, drive this truck, write this report, or paint this wall; I *get* to."

The other night I found myself saying, "I have to take out the garbage." And I thought of a dear friend in a wheelchair who would love to take out the garbage tonight. He hasn't been able to since that awful day one January.

I get to. I'm so blessed.

The central message of the Bible can be summed up in three words: God so loved. "God so loved the world," says John 3:16, "that he gave his one and only Son, that whoever believes in him shall not perish but have eternal life" (NIV).

Is it possible to make someone smile with three words? I think so. Start here:

- Why so serious?
- Greater is he.
- Why so fearful?
- Nothing is impossible.

- Why so downcast?
- Hope in God.
- He is risen.
- We are loved.
- Love never fails.
- Love conquers all.
- All is well.
- Thank you, Lord.

13

Big Baby

 I'm not absolutely certain of this, but someone needs to look into it. I think all flu bugs are the result of little kids trying to blow out birthday candles.

When we are out of sympathy with the young, then I think our work in this world is over.

GEORGE MACDONALD

Have you heard this one? One summer night during a severe thunderstorm, a mother tucked her small son into bed. She was about to turn off the light when he asked in a trembling voice, "Mommy, will you stay with me all night?"

Smiling, the mother gave him a warm, reassuring hug. "I can't, dear. I have to sleep in Daddy's room."

There was silence. Then the little guy said, "The big baby!"

Fear. Do you have some?

We just spent the weekend with five grandbabies aged three and under, thanks to kids who entrust them to us and who have been prolific in the Having Children department. Two hours with this many grandchildren will leave you energized. Two days with them will leave you exhausted.

The Bible says that on the seventh day God rested. Perhaps it was because the toddlers had yet to arrive. I have come to believe that it is a very good thing God did not allow us to have babies of our own at my stage of life. Not just because we might forget where we placed them, but because by Monday morning you cannot bend over and touch your toes. If you see older people holding grand-children and wearing faraway looks, it is because all they hear is, "Carry me. Throw me. Catch me. Again. Again. Now…ice cream." Be nice to these people. They can't tie their own shoes. That's why they wear flip-flops.

The truth is, I am wild about these grandkids. They have taught me what true love means. It means watching *Paw Patrol* while base-ball is on another channel.

Now, Claira is two and calls me "Bubba." Long blonde curls bounce behind her as she walks, and she has the attention span of a gnat. Claira likes to move quickly, like an unknotted balloon, to find new items and shake the stuffing out of them.

Dismantling things is her spiritual gift. She celebrated turning three by dismantling her bed. I kid you not. She may be a mechanic one day, if at some point she learns how to locate the parts and reas-semble them. Like a hummingbird, she flits about with wide-eyed optimism and a toothy grin.

The girl seems fearless too. But as we ate breakfast in a restau-rant on Saturday, wondering what possessed us to agree to such a thing, I noticed Claira leaning to one side, looking past me. I turned to look in that direction. A very large and dark closet was staring straight at us.

"Mooheee," she said. I removed her soother. She repeated herself, this time enunciating, "Monkey."

She kept leaning, wide eyed, ogling the closet. I made a mon-key sound. Her eyes grew wider. "Monkey," she said, pointing at the closet.

She hadn't eaten a thing. She reached for me. I held her close and walked toward the darkness. Claira wriggled and fought me all the way. The child in me wanted to say, "There are no monkeys. The tigers ate them all." The grandpa in me said, "Monkeys are fun, Claira. What's his name?" I knelt down on the floor beside her and answered my own question. "His name is E.E. He's a nice monkey. He likes Claira."

She enjoyed this more than I thought she would. She smiled. She laughed. We said goodbye to E.E. and enjoyed our breakfast.

Around 11:00 a.m. we put her down for a nap. I've never been comfortable with the phrase "put her down," but that's what we did, I suppose. She said, "Nubbamababa." I removed her soother. She repeated herself: "Nuggamebubba."

"Pardon me?" *Nuggamebubba?* And then I recalled what her mama told me. She likes to snuggle. "Snuggle me, Bubba." And that's what I did, stroking her golden curls while this precious child drifted off to sleep.

Fear. Do you have some?

Perhaps this is what God says to you today: "I've got this. Nothing will get to you that didn't get past me first. Fear not. I am with you. Be not dismayed. I am your God. Replace that fear with a confident gratitude that you are my precious child. And snuggle in."

Sunday night we somehow managed to return the children to their rightful owners, and as we slipped off our flip-flops, we couldn't stop smiling. Each time after the grandchildren leave, I have a warm feeling. I think it means the extra strength Tiger Balm is kicking in.

14

God and the Giant Veggies

 I heard a little kid say something very wise.
"Grown-ups should skip more instead of walking.
Then they wouldn't be so grumpy."

It is impossible on reasonable grounds
to disbelieve miracles.

BLAISE PASCAL

A farmer purchased an abandoned farm. The house was falling apart. Fences were broken down. The fields were overgrown with weeds. One day the town preacher stopped by to bless the man's work, saying, "May God and you work together to make this the farm of your dreams."

Six months passed. The preacher returned. The once dilapidated farmhouse was completely rebuilt. Broken-down fences now housed livestock happily munching grass. The fields were filled with crops planted in neat rows.

"Amazing!" said the preacher. "Look what God and you have accomplished together!"

"Yes, Reverend," said the farmer, "but remember what the farm was like when God was working it alone!"

The farmer in this joke reminds me of Jimmy Stewart's character in the movie *Shenandoah*. He plays a wealthy but crusty widower who farms the land and opposes the American Civil War on moral grounds. One night before the conflict hits home, Stewart gathers his sons around the dinner table and prays, "Lord, we cleared this land. We plowed it, sowed it, and harvested. We cooked the harvest. It wouldn't be here, we wouldn't be eatin' it, if we hadn't done it all ourselves. We worked dog-bone hard for every crumb and morsel. But we thank you just the same anyway, Lord, for this food we're about to eat. Amen."

Contrast that kind of prayer with the mealtime prayers of kids. We'll start with my granddaughter Sophie: "Dear Jesus, thank you that Daddy is strong and Mommy makes this food. No thank you for the onions."

Ricky, age four, said, "Dear God, Thanks that my dog eats the food I don't want."

And this is from Eugene, age five: "Dear God, I didn't think orange went with purple until I saw the sunset you made on Tuesday. That was cool."

We do our part, but without a creator capable of riotously extravagant sunsets, there would be nothing from which to start. If you doubt me, try growing carrots from scratch. Let me know how it goes.

The people of Almolonga agree. Located in the cool highlands of Guatemala, this city of 17,000 was once ravaged by poverty, fear, and violence. Alcoholism was rampant. A stroll through town in the morning meant stepping over men passed out on the street. Overflow prisoners were bussed to a nearby city from Almolonga's four jam-packed prisons.

Times were dark. Idols and ancestral spirits were worshipped. Christians were a despised minority. Preachers were chased away with sticks and rocks. One day a local pastor, Mariano Riscajahé, was abducted by six men, and a gun barrel was shoved down his throat. Mariano silently prayed for protection. A man pulled the trigger. The gun clicked but didn't go off.

Mariano called his small congregation together to fast and pray day and night. Each Saturday they held a prayer vigil for their community. And things began to change. Men vacated bars and came to church. Many cut ties with the spirits they feared. Churches grew. Lives changed. The crime rate declined.

Before long, the last of Almolonga's four prisons was closed.

Today, locals insist that as the spiritual state changed, the land changed too. Talk about climate change. As people were set free, they began working the land more efficiently and harvesting bumper crops. Growers once exported four truckloads of vegetables a month. Today, their payload exceeds 40 trucks a week—a 900% increase.

When reporters and researchers drop by to find out why the town's veggies are so big, they find carrots the size of a man's forearm and grinning farmers who give the credit to God.

"God had nothing to do with it," skeptics say. "It's just better farming principles." But few can argue that it isn't just the veggies that have been altered. The town of Almolonga is a stunning picture of the transforming power of the gospel of Jesus Christ.

Now, I'm not a come-to-Jesus-and-your-veggies-will-explode kind of guy. Some of the most robust faith I have encountered is among friends in Central America who live in poverty. "[The Father] sends rain on the just and the unjust alike," said Jesus.[1] But God also promised, "If my people, who are called by my name, will humble themselves and pray and seek my face and turn from their wicked ways, then I will hear from heaven, and I will forgive their sin and will heal their land" (2 Chronicles 7:14 NIV).

Over and over the Bible tells us that our heavenly Father longs to pour out his blessing on those who love him, until there won't be room enough to store it all.[2] May God give us the faith of a child—the faith to take care of the small stuff and watch him take care of the rest.

Speaking of children, I can't end this chapter without a bedtime prayer from little Sophie.

> *Dear God, thank you for my best mommy and daddy in the whole world who take care of me. Thank you for you. Please send your angels to watch over Jesus, too, because he takes care of all of us.*

15

What's His Name?

 I am convinced that some people put more thought into choosing their Wi-Fi password than naming their child.

The God to whom little boys say their prayers
has a face very like their mother's.

J.M. BARRIE

can't tell you how excited I was the first time my granddaughter called me "Bumpa." Then I discovered she calls everything "Bumpa." A tomato. Trees. She points at a block of Gouda cheese and says, "Bumpa." A friend's grandchild calls him "Gramma" and sometimes "Grumpy," so I figure I don't have it so bad.

Names are interesting.

My mother named me Philip. My friends called me "Gertrude," thanks to older brothers who dubbed me thus when I was three. In seventh grade my teacher wrote the nickname on my report card, and my mother became so concerned about correcting my teacher that she completely forgot about my grades. What a blessing.

Mom loved my name. She once told me she started thinking of it months before I was born. Scribbled it on a slip of paper. Tried it out on friends. Whispered it to me when I was in the womb and in my ear when I was an infant. Mom rocked me to sleep singing impromptu songs with my name in them, like "Rock-a-Bye Philip" and "Twinkle, Twinkle, Little Phil." When I was older she even had it embroidered on a tie-dye T-shirt for a birthday present.

So it's amazing that half the time when I was growing up she had no idea who I was.

She would start to call me but couldn't remember my name at all. She called me by my siblings' names: Dan, Dave, Tim, Ruth, and sometimes Inky, which was our snarly little terrier's name. I'm sure some kids are traumatized by this. I thought it was more fun than a closet full of kittens. Of course I went through a bit of an identity crisis there for a while when she called me "Smarten Up" and "Get in Here! You Know Who You Are!" For one entire week I thought my name was Fiddlesticks.

Mothers with more than two children are just glad if they can remember why they called you in the first place. The Walters family lived down the road a ways. Their kids were named Anne, Dan, Stan, Jan, and Fran—and once they'd exhausted the alphabet, along came little Thomas. Imagine calling them for supper.

My wife sometimes calls our children by her siblings' names: Janice, Dennis, LaVerne, Caroline, Miriam, and Cynthia. They got used to it in time.

"I'm Rachael," my daughter once informed my wife. "Say it with me, Mom: Rachael."

"What did I call you?"

"You called me Rex. That was your dog when you were little."

Ramona smiled. "I always liked Rex."

The more the family extends, the worse it gets. Jeff married Rae-lyn. Jordan married Rachael. It's too many *J*'s and *R*'s. We pray for them each night and often start laughing because we get the couples mixed up. I'm quite certain God can sort it all out. He must smile a lot listening to our prayers.

Few comforts are greater in hard times than knowing there is one who never forgets our names. Listen to these promises from the Bible.

- In John 10, Jesus compares himself to a shepherd who calls his sheep by name. "I am the good shepherd," he says, "I know my own and my own know me" (verse 14 ESV).

- In Exodus 33, God tells Moses, "This very thing that you have spoken I will do, for you have found favor in my sight, and I know you by name" (verse 17 ESV). I like that. In Isaiah 43, the Lord reminds the people of Israel, "Fear not, for I have redeemed you; I have called you by name, you are mine" (verse 1 ESV).

- In Matthew 10, Jesus says, "Are not two sparrows sold for a penny? And not one of them will fall to the ground apart from your Father. But even the hairs of your head are all numbered. Fear not, therefore; you are of more value than many sparrows" (verses 29-31 ESV).

- In Isaiah 49, God says, "See, I have written your name on the palms of my hands" (verse 16). He also asks, "Can a mother forget her nursing child?...Even if that were possible, I would not forget you!" (verse 15).

Mom forgot my name, but never once did I doubt that she loved me. Getting names right just wasn't her spiritual gift. I once asked her why she called me by a friend's name, and she laughed. "I guess I should pass out name tags at breakfast," she said. "You'll understand one day." And I do now.

One Saturday when my son was small, he had his jammies on inside out. I called him Fruit of the Loom for two days.

Part 2

Live Without Regret

 I just celebrated another birthday. I said to Ramona, "I'm getting so old I don't even know what to wear. I mean, do I wear boxers or briefs?" She said, "Uh…well. Depends."

f you've ever typed words into a device, you've encountered auto-correct—perhaps with hilarious residue. I mean results.

One guy sent a text to a friend, "I sold my Grandma for $2,000." He meant "Grand Am car."

Then there's this texting conversation: "I start my new job with the police force Thursday. Just picked up my new unicorn." "Wow!" said a friend, "You get your own unicorn? Best job ever." "Uniform! Uniform!"

Someone confessed, "The whole office is complaining because I have tuna in my underwear." Who could blame them? "Tupper-ware!" he retyped carefully, then pushed the send button.

Have you ever wished for something that fixes your mistakes before you make them? We've all said things we'd like to take back. Rephrase. Blot out. I've written things I've regretted. Graceless things. I've needed forgiveness. As did the wife who texted her husband, "Happy birthday, dead husband…" I think she meant *dear*.

A guy got a large tattoo that says, "No Regerts." Well, I think he has one now. If we're honest, so do we.

Did Jesus have regrets? Perhaps. He called twelve men to follow him, and one by one they let him down. Yet he turned eleven of them into the greatest purveyors of good news ever. Can regrets be turned into residue? I mean rejoicing? Our answer begins in a prison not far from my hometown.

> If you, Lord, kept a record of sins...who could stand?
> But with you there is forgiveness,
> so that we can, with reverence, serve you.
>
> **PSALM 130:3-4 NIV**

16

Miracle in Cell Block 3

 I've never stolen anything from a store. Honest. But when I leave without buying something, I always think, *Take your hands out of your pockets and don't dart your eyes. You're innocent.*

Let me be thankful, first, because he never robbed me before; second, because although he took my purse, he did not take my life; third, because although he took all I possessed, it was not much; and fourth, because it was I who was robbed, not I who robbed.

MATTHEW HENRY

was sentenced to prison on Sunday. For about three hours. And it wasn't a sentence, but an invitation to speak to inmates. A "captive audience," you might say.

Visiting prison is one of those opportunities that initially scared me half to death. Blame prison movies if you like, but a hundred trips to the principal's office gave me an aversion to razor wire, high walls, and armed guards. In high school, a teacher warned me that I'd end up in prison if I didn't wise up, smarten up, and grow up. And I have no doubt he was right.

Entering the chapel, I watched a heavily whiskered inmate push his wheelchair over to me and stop. Two decades ago I had read his front-page story. He reached out a hand, grinned, and reeled off a litany of one-liners. "If you're ever attacked by a bunch of circus clowns," he said, "go for the juggler." He was just getting warmed up. "Did you know that the world tongue-twister champion just got arrested? They're gonna give him a really tough sentence." Before I could get the joke, he was on to another: "I woke up this morning and forgot what side the sun rises on. Then it dawned on me."

I laughed, but I also wondered, *How do you laugh when regret haunts you every day? How do you tell jokes when you've been locked up for 20 years, and the next 20 don't look so bright?* I asked, "How can you be all right when everything's wrong?"

He pointed to the floor, and his eyes misted over. "This room," he said. Before I had time to ask what he meant, Bart, a convict who coordinates the prison chapels, was pulling me toward the front. Bart leads a study group for ten dads who are learning how to be better husbands and fathers; how to hold each other accountable; how to be men of integrity. All are federal inmates; most are violent offenders.

Just before Christmas, Bart decided to organize a fundraiser. So he asked Gord, a musician friend of mine on the outside, to put a band together and play the great tunes of Christmas. His group of ten spread the word. They hoped 30 would show up. But the inmates blew the doors off. Not literally, but they sat in the aisles; they lined the walls.

When I heard of a fundraiser in prison, my first thought was, *Are you out of your mind?*

"Brothers," Bart began, "we have a lot to be thankful for."

Like what? I thought. *Hard bunks? Bad food? Mean guards?*

"We have a roof over our heads every night," Bart went on, oblivious to the irony.

Someone yelled, "Something to eat every day."

I thought there would be laughter, but he was serious.

Bart leaned forward, rubbing his hands. "There are some families in a nearby town. They're poor. The kids won't have Christmas gifts. Let's help them. Let's take an offering."

Pardon me? An offering? How do you take up a collection in prison? These guys are forbidden from carrying cash. Those with jobs can earn up to four bucks a day. It's like expecting silence from a toddler. Impossible. Still, clipboards with transfer forms were passed out.

How much could they raise? Twenty bucks? Thirty?

When the forms were added up, the inmates celebrated. They had donated $1,000 to needy families. Like the woman in the Bible who put in a few pennies while the rich ceremoniously gave grander amounts, these men brought a smile to God's face that night. Jesus said of that widow, "[She] has put more into the treasury than all the others. They all gave out of their wealth; but she, out of her poverty, put in everything—all she had to live on."[1]

My friend in the wheelchair makes it clear. Joy comes in looking beyond our situation, no matter how bleak, and somehow helping others. Holocaust survivor Viktor Frankl wrote, "Everything can be taken from a man but one thing: the last of the human freedoms—to choose one's attitude in any given set of circumstances."[2]

And so I stood and confessed to the inmates my own ingratitude and asked what else they were thankful for. One said, "A family that's praying for me."

"You," said another. "I need to laugh."

"Who gave thanks to God for prison food?" I ask. A tattooed hand goes up. "Wow," is all I can say. He is one of those amazing people you meet who counts his problems, then counts his blessings. If the problems outnumber the blessings, he counts again.

Another hand is thrust upward. It's the joker in the wheelchair. "I'm thankful for prison," he says. "I met Jesus here."

I can't talk for a minute on account of the lump in my throat. Everything has been taken from him—except the last of our freedoms. To choose his attitude when he can't go back; to choose his attitude when he can't choose his circumstances. "God has done amazing things in your life, hasn't he?" I finally manage.

"Oh yeah," he nods.

There were smiles. High fives. And laughter born of sincere gratitude that can't be explained or faked.

We'll find miracles great and small, if we go looking. For me, few have surpassed that Christmas miracle in cell block 3.

17

The Bad Old Days

If you survived the '60s, you're a miracle. Everyone smoked. Little kids smoked. Cats smoked. Dogs smoked. The guy pumping gas smoked—cigarette in one hand, gas nozzle in the other. It's a wonder we weren't all blown to kingdom come.

Every age has consisted of crises that seemed intolerable to the people who lived through them.

BROOKS ATKINSON

was grocery shopping when an older guy passed me in a bit of rush. We sometimes play golf together, so I asked, "Where are you going?"

"To the coffee shop," he said.

"What do you guys do there?"

He stopped, smiled, and hiked his eyebrows a bit. "We gripe; we complain."

I loved his honesty. "What do you talk about?"

"The good old days."

How could I disagree? I miss 25-cent ice cream cones that were too big to eat. I miss having time for a bubble bath on Saturday night. I was youngest, so the water was clean.

But the coffee guy wasn't done. "We talk about how bad things are. Politics. Teenagers. Music."

I nodded. "Yeah. Sometimes it sounds like someone's trying to kill chickens with a jackhammer. But you know something? The good old days weren't all good."

He frowned. "What do you mean?"

"Well, remember when you had to wait three minutes for your tube radio to warm up?"

He grinned. "Yup."

"Remember when you had to wade through six feet of ugly green shag carpet to change one channel on the TV?"

He grinned wider.

"You sent your little brother up onto the roof to adjust the antenna, didn't you? In the dead of winter with a howling north wind. 'Hold it right there!' you said. 'I think that's *Star Trek*. Or it could be *Lawrence Welk*. Lick the pole.' "

He laughed. "That's about all we had on TV," he said. "That and snow." And we stood there talking about the way it was.

How we had to wash dishes with soap and water. How we learned to dance while our brothers flicked our hind quarters with towels. We had to remember phone numbers. And look up information in five-pound encyclopedias. Lick stamps. Mail letters. Roll down car windows. And lift garage doors. There was no delete key on typewriters—just little bottles of Wite-Out. Phones were attached to walls. It took about a minute to dial any given number. Our phone had a three-foot cord. If your girlfriend called, everyone in the room could hear every word you said. Your sister stood right behind you while you talked. And made gagging noises. No, the good old days were not all good.

We were laughing like little kids now. People were worried about us.

"Times are tough," I said. "But they're the only times we're given."

I told him of a friend who lost his house to a horrendous fire.

How his church gathered around him. I told him of the 18-year-old who said, "I was raised atheist. My parents gave me no hope, no purpose, no meaning, no joy. But I rebelled and found them all in Jesus."

I told him what my pastor friend in China told me. That rumors are spreading. There are more Christians than Communists there now. And thousands are coming to faith in Jesus in the Middle East. "God is doing a new thing. Right now. Today."

I told him that much of what we see depends on what we go looking for. That I love FaceTime with the grandkids and heated car seats and GPS. "I never mastered how to fold a road map," I admitted.

"Me neither," he said.

"Try talking this way in the coffee shop and see what happens."

"They'll think I'm crazy, you know. I can't wait."

Of course I miss some things.

I miss ten-cent ice cream cones.

I miss milk delivery when the cream rose to the top.

I miss sleeping with the blinds up so I could wake with the sun and play outside.

I miss not really caring if my socks matched at all.

I miss having no idea who paid the bills.

I miss walking down the street, holding dad's hand—and no one finding it odd.

I miss the taste of candy before someone warned that it would kill me.

I miss having just one phone per family, though long-distance calls were $5 a minute.

I miss evenings when everyone and their cat was out for a walk or playing ball.

Ecclesiastes 7:10 says, "Do not say, 'Why were the old days better than these?' For it is not wise to ask such questions" (NIV). So how do we look back? "I remember the days of old," writes the psalmist. "I meditate on all that you have done; I ponder the work of your hands."[1] The wise look back and remember with gratitude what God has done.

Years ago in Sacramento, California, a ticket agent inadvertently oversold a Women of Faith weekend event by 1,500 seats. It was a wee bit of a problem. So they exchanged the chairs on the main floor for smaller, plastic ones. The setup looked a bit like a boxing match, chairs right up to the stage. Many would have to crane their necks like those in the front row at the movies. Organizers phoned *all* the ladies beforehand to alert them, then reseated them Friday night, apologizing profusely.

But before long the complaints arrived. Some were uncomfortable. Some were angry. So organizers asked the next speaker if she would mind apologizing again on behalf of the organizers. She agreed.

Her name is Joni Eareckson Tada. She is a quadriplegic, paralyzed as a teenager from a diving accident. Her story is one of triumph—even joy—amid the trials of paralysis.

Wheeled onto the platform, this is what Joni said:

"I understand some of you are not sitting in the chairs you expected to be sitting in tonight. Well, neither am I. And I've been in mine for more than thirty years." Then she added softly, "I have at least a thousand friends who would give anything to be sitting in the chair you are in if only for tonight."

A hush fell over the room. No one complained after that. In fact, many said it was one of the most memorable events of their life.[2]

So it is when we overflow with gratitude. This is *the* great secret of the joy-filled life.

May we look back to remember what God has done. And look not on what we do not have, but on what God has given us. May we spend more time looking up than looking back. Even if the coffee shop patrons think we're crazy.

18

Oh, Leon

 One day my daughter showed me a picture she drew of me. "I was trying to draw Mommy," she said, "but I messed up."

> I have not failed. I have just found
> 10,000 ways that won't work.
>
> **THOMAS A. EDISON**

Few things coax a smile to my face as quickly as watching sports bloopers. A baseball outfielder loses track of a fly ball; it bounces off his head and over the fence: home run. A college player leaps to catch a football, collides with the mascot, and they land in someone's drink.

I love sports bloopers because I've caused a few myself. In overtime during a championship hockey game, I once scored a goal—into my own team's net. I've missed the hoop, tripped over my cleats, and fallen off a ski lift. I'm the only one I know who has dropped barbells on his nose. I don't want to talk about it.

Nor does Leon Lett Jr.

If you were a Dallas Cowboys fan in the '90s, you won't soon forget Leon. He was a great football player, but his name has been memorialized, not for his great plays (and they were many), but for his on-field blunders.

In Super Bowl XXVII, while playing against the Buffalo Bills, Leon recovered a late-game fumble on the Dallas 35-yard line and took off running. As he approached the goal line, he slowed down and held the ball out in celebration, unaware that Bills' player Don Beebe was chasing him down. Beebe stripped the ball from Leon's outstretched hand, costing him the touchdown.

Later, Leon sheepishly admitted that he took his eyes off the goal. He had been watching the jumbotron, trying to copy a trademark Michael Irvin play where Michael held the ball out across the goal line.

But Leon wasn't finished.

The following season on Thanksgiving Day, during a rare Dallas snowstorm, the Cowboys led the Miami Dolphins 14–13. Fifteen seconds remained. The Dolphins lined up to attempt a 41-yard field goal to take the lead. But the kick was blocked. The ball bounced and rolled, then stopped, spinning in the snow as the seconds ticked down. The Cowboys had the lead; the victory was theirs. All they had to do was keep from touching the ball. Easy enough.

But out of nowhere came Leon Lett. He sprinted toward the ball. He lost his footing and slid, knocking the ball toward a Miami player, who recovered it on the one-yard line. Miami attempted another field goal and won the game 16–14.

A few weeks later, Leon received a letter from a young girl who hoped to console him. "Leon," she wrote, "don't worry about it. Last year during the Super Bowl there was a guy that was going in to score a touchdown and had the ball ripped out of his hand right before he scored. So it's okay, people make mistakes all the time."

Leon just sat there shaking his head.

The little girl had no idea that, too, had been Leon.

And what is he up to now? Wait a few paragraphs, and I'll tell you the rest of the story.

First, I hope you have a soft spot in your heart for Leon. I do. If we're honest, we can relate. We've messed up. Not before millions of fans perhaps, but we've fallen short. Failed. Done things we've regretted.

Then along comes Jesus. He says to Matthew, "Hey, follow me. Not as you wish you were. Just as you are."

"Uh, but Jesus, I'm a tax collector. People hate me."

"I can work with that."[1]

He says to Saul, "Follow me."

"Uh, but Jesus, I've been arresting Christians. It's, uh, how I make a living. I'd like to murder your followers."

"Tell you what. I'll change your name to Paul and use you to turn the world upside down. Follow me."[2]

I don't know if Paul was an athlete like Leon, but in Philippians 3 he used athletic terms when he wrote, "I focus on this one thing: Forgetting the past and looking forward to what lies ahead, I press on to reach the end of the race and receive the heavenly prize for which God, through Christ Jesus, is calling us."[3]

When success comes, we give thanks. When failure comes, we seek God's grace.

Live this way, and you are no longer defined by your mistakes or messes. After all, God can teach us through failure what we will never learn through success. And true success can't be measured in touchdowns or contracts or ratings or money, but in simply getting to know God better and pressing on.

I think Leon would agree that you're never finished until you quit. And what is he up to now? Well, Leon understood that failure is never a dead end; it's a detour. He is now an assistant coach with the Dallas Cowboys. When asked about the fumbles, he's able to laugh. And on the twentieth anniversary of that unforgettable day when Don Beebe stripped the ball away, Leon turned the notorious into the victorious. He went and celebrated with Beebe himself.[4]

19

#Selfie-Centered

 I'm so old I can remember that time when
I went without my cell phone for 42 years.

Home is where the heart is, but today,
the phone is where the heart is.
RACHITHA CABRAL

When I was a kid, before phones took pictures, good snap shots of yourself were rare. No one took selfies in those days. You couldn't afford them. You bought film and mailed it away to be developed. Sometimes half the pictures returned completely black because the camera malfunctioned. Of the rest, two might be of your eyebrow.

Whenever Grandpa Callaway visited, he packed a camera and a box of flashbulbs that almost never flashed. We spent half of Christmas Day trying to get one good family picture. We'd get all dressed up, slick back our hair with Vaseline, smile widely as Grandpa clicked the shutter and—nothing. The flashbulb wouldn't flash. "Oh say," he'd mutter. Then he'd pull out the bulb, shake it, study it, lick it, and cram it back in. Then the flash would go off while the camera was pointed at a lampshade.

And so it is that I love new technology.

One day my son caught me reading a book and told me of something called Facebook. I thought, *That's the dumbest idea since the pogo stick. It'll never fly.* He said, "I'm on it. My friends are too."

I said, "Sign me up."

He helped me create an account, which was like showing your grandpa how to operate a microwave. "Just open this door and put the potato in. No, Gramps. The potato. Not your dentures. Then set the time. No, you just put it on high for 500 minutes. You'll nuke the house."

With Facebook, my phone became a welcome companion. It connected me with old friends, helped me organize a backyard football game, and even cheered people up. "We're out buying Christmas gifts for the kids," I posted. "We're spending their inheritance." Friends would comment and "like" what I said. I was flattered.

I began to count likes and comments. Suddenly, I had 5,000 friends. I did the math. That's 13.7 birthday parties to attend each day. Thankfully, I found that "friend" didn't mean that much anymore. No commitment. No chocolate. No dropping by the house.

Still, I loved FaceTime with my daughter on my phone. Taking selfies until I got them just right. No more flashbulbs for me. I did find it easier to be self-absorbed, however. A real friend who lived two doors away showed me a study. Four out of five social media posts are about one topic:

Me.

We are now certifiably selfie-centered. "Hey, everybody! Enough about you. Let's talk about me!" We get positive affirmation from our posts, and our brains release dopamine, a legalized drug that delivers a buzz and addicts us to—ourselves. According to Tim Elmore, president of Growing Leaders, the average adolescent would sooner lose a pinkie finger than their cell phone.[1]

I didn't understand this—until one night, home alone, the unthinkable happened. I lost my phone. I panicked. I mean, what if someone texted me? What if I missed a phone call? A post? A like?

An email? Worse, what if my Twitter followers had forgotten me? What then?

My phone had become my teddy bear.

Finally, I found it. In my back pocket. Dead. Before plugging it in, I sat down to have a talk with myself.

"You're living for likes," I said.

"That's a bit harsh," I replied.

"Maybe. But sometimes I think you care more about what others think than what God thinks."

"Ouch."

"If idols are things we want more than God, then 'ouch' is right. I think you should go forty days without social media and see what happens to you."

And so I did.

Here is what I discovered.

It's possible.

For the first few days I had the shakes. Then I began keeping a journal, which included these highlights:

- "Each previous generation in world history has lived without these gizmos. Maybe I can."

- "I am having more face-to-face conversations with real friends, uninterrupted by the ding of a phone."

- "I have stopped plunging down so many ADHD rabbit holes that lead nowhere profitable."

- "My 'comparitometer' isn't jumping off the charts."

- "I am more likely to care about what God thinks than what others think."

- "This fast has made me hungrier for God. For time with him. For time considering his words."

- "Found this today: 'Look carefully then how you walk, not as unwise but as wise, making the best use of the time, because the days are evil' (Ephesians 5:15-16 ESV)."

- "The only downside? Ramona saw I had extra time and asked me to do some stuff."

It's profitable.

I'm not for revisiting the flashbulb, but if we want our joy and sanity and kids back, more visits, phone calls, and actual face time could be the start. These technological tools can be used to encourage and build up others. I will continue doing that. But a good thing should never become an ultimate thing.

In Costco I overheard a boy say to his mother, "You like your phone more than me." Our phones have replaced our alarm clock, camera, CD player, and calendar. May they never replace our family.

It's a popular thing to say, "I live with no regrets." At the same time, we spend almost four hours a day on our mobile devices.[2] We check our phones 52 times a day.[3] Trust me, we will regret that one day.

We've all seen it happen. A family of four is texting one another in a restaurant. It's like watching a train wreck. Maybe they're texting mom what they want to eat, so she can send a tweet to the waiter. More likely, they could use a cyber fast like I did. For me, it all started with the question, "Am I using these gizmos for good or letting them master me?"

Now, when I'm out for a meal with family or friends, we have an agreement. First one to fish out their device picks up the check.

20

Parenting Tips

 Ever drop a pacifier on the floor? With our first child, I sterilized the thing. With our third child, I blew on it and wiped it on my sleeve.

I don't remember who said this, but there really are places in the heart you don't even know exist until you love a child.
ANNE LAMOTT

Without a doubt, parenting is one of the most frustrating, heart-stopping, expensive, and rewarding privileges you will ever have. But then you snap your fingers, and your youngest turns 30, like our Jeff does this Saturday. We can't turn the clock back. Would we do some things different? Sure. But wise parents go easy on themselves. Remember how exhausted we were? Our kids arrived with no mute buttons and no guarantees. To complicate matters, we were rookies. By the time we became experts, we were unemployed.

So we learned to laugh.

We did what we could to build bridges.

We give thanks for three well-adjusted, grown-up kids.

And we smile about the parenting tips we've picked up along the way. Here are just 30. I hope they make you smile too.

1. "Never lend your car to anyone to whom you have given birth."[1]

2. At some point all great parents deal with regret, so remember this: God says, "I forgive you." So forgive yourself. Unless your standards are higher than his.

3. Laugh together. I used to collect and tell jokes at the dinner table. Sometimes they were lame, like this one: Why does a chicken coop always have two doors? Because if it had four doors, it would be a chicken sedan.

4. Raise kids with real face time.

5. Model the behavior you want your kids to embrace.

6. Let your kids catch you being kind and friendly—even goofy—with strangers. I bought ice cream and milk at the grocery store and said to the lady at checkout, "I'm lactose intolerant; are these a good choice?" She said, "After seven hours on my feet, I needed that." My daughter smiled for ten minutes.

7. A word to you young couples: Even in the best of families, there's the risk that a baby could be born. Do not panic. Borrow money from your parents.

8. Find a child's strengths and encourage them.

9. Tell your children when things make you laugh. For example, I saw a flashing sign at a tire store. They were having a "Blowout Sale." I snapped a picture and sent it to the kids.

10. Remember, whatever is true, honorable, right, pure, lovely, and of good report (Philippians 4:8) likely won't be found on the news.

11. Husbands, beware. Ramona told me, "I love you. Take me shopping." It was a trick.

12. When we got back from shopping I told Ramona, "Honey, I don't think there's anything I wouldn't do for you. Except the dishes." I'm kidding. Do the dishes.

13. Shut off the TV every chance you get. Television is called a medium because it's seldom rare or well done.

14. Never say this in an argument with your spouse: "If it makes you feel better, I'll pretend I'm wrong."

15. Never gossip about your kids. Make sure every child is safe in a room when he or she is not in it. Unless you're talking about what he's getting for Christmas.

16. One of the most powerful gifts you can give is your attention. Every child is loved. Every child is more important than your phone.

17. Let your kids see you laugh today. Kids see our joy and never quite get over it.

18. I said to my wife, "I do not have ADHD! I'm just easily distrac—"

19. A tip for enjoying family time in the summer: Raise the lid *before* igniting the barbecue.

20. Your children don't need to watch movies while you drive. Allow them to be bored sometimes. Thriving brain cells develop this way.

21. Clean the kitchen together. The best way to keep your kids out of hot water is to put some dishes in it.

22. Remember that every family faces a crisis. And the only way to face a crisis is together.

23. Let your kids catch you necking. With your spouse, of course. If you don't know what necking is, ask an old person.

24. Let your kids catch you reading the Bible and praying.

25. Eat together.

26. Listen first. Talk second.

27. Read together. Pray together. Memorize Bible verses together.

28. Make sure your life and lips line up. Proverbs 20:7 says, "The righteous who walks in his integrity— blessed are his children after him!" (ESV).

29. They say love doesn't last. Neither does deodorant. That's why we put it on every day.

30. When your kids turn out great, be humble about it. The world could use more humble people. There are so few of us left.

21

My Very Own Time Machine

You may not know this, but I was voted "Most Likely to Build a Time Machine" by the Class of 2314.

Reflect upon your present blessings—of which every man has many—not on your past misfortunes, of which all men have some.

CHARLES DICKENS

n 1969 man first walked on the moon. Big deal. That was the year I became the first 8-year-old boy to successfully experience time travel.

Compton's Encyclopedia first informed me of the theory, suggesting that in order to travel back in time, I would have to make something go faster than the speed of light. Intrigued, I stripped my brother's Golden Hawk three-speed bicycle of its mud flaps. I oiled the chain and hubs for aerodynamics. I pushed that bike to the top of the highest of a series of very low hills on Canada's western prairie—a hill so high my father could place our car in neutral and hit 30 miles an hour halfway down without even removing the mud flaps.

I confidently climbed aboard that three-speed. Secured a small hockey helmet to my pointy head. Affixed my sister's pink-rimmed sunglasses to my face. Gave that bike a shove and pedaled like a gopher being chased by a coonhound.

I'll spare you the violent details of the next 38 seconds of my life, but let's just say that instead of traveling through time and finding myself in the past, I traveled about a quarter mile through gravel at the speed of "scream," skidded through a shallow ditch on my keister, and stopped inches from a barbed wire fence. I had indeed entered another dimension.

The rest of that day is still a little fuzzy. I do recall a rather blurry-looking nurse asking me a question as she filled out a report. Something about "cause of accident." I believe I answered, "Time travel experiment," though I'm sure she wrote down other things. Things like, "You can't pay me enough to work here...I recommend we forget about his arm and examine his head."

Over a cup of coffee, I recently recounted this story for a friend. He laughed, then asked a question I hadn't thought of since that fateful day: "Where would you go if you had your very own time machine?"

I didn't know. "Maybe to 1975," I said. "Zip on over to Albuquerque, get to know Billy Gates, scoop up some Microsoft shares. Or maybe I would travel back to that time in high school when my friends dared me to eat six burritos in one sitting, only this time I would avoid those fateful words, 'Why not?'"

I asked him where *he* would go if he had a time machine. His answer caught me a little off guard. "I'd travel back about eight years. I'd humble myself. I'd forgive my wife." Like all of us, he had failed. Pressed down by the weight of his past, he was unable to cherish the present.

In an airport one day, a flight attendant asked me, "Would you like to check your baggage?" and I laughed. "Yeah," I said. "I've got some baggage I'd like to check." She knew exactly what I meant. Most of us lug around burdens God never intended for us to carry.

Regret can be an appalling waste of time and energy unless it causes us to do three things.

Make it right.

Few things foster regret like the weight of our own sin. Two verses can change everything: "If we confess our sins, he is faithful and just to forgive us our sins and to cleanse us from all unrighteousness" (1 John 1:9 ESV), and, "There is therefore now no condemnation for those who are in Christ Jesus" (Romans 8:1 ESV).

As surely as my mom used to lick a hankie and scrub assorted guck from my five-year-old face, God says, "Here. Let me handle that. No matter how deep the stain, I can take it out."[1]

At its best, regret awakens us to that which needs to be changed, made right, or done better.

Trace God's hand.

Lengthy portions of the Bible are exclusively reserved for remembering God's hand on history. "Remember what the LORD your God did..." says Deuteronomy 7:18 (ESV). "I recall all you have done, O LORD; I remember your wonderful deeds of long ago," says Psalm 77:11. The wise look back only to recall God's faithfulness, to reflect on his mercy and grace.

Some speak of Karma, that the sum of our actions will determine our fate, that we get what we deserve. Grace says, "No. You get what you can never deserve: God's love. God's favor. God's forgiveness." May we remember this every day.

Give thanks.

Gratitude is good, but it must always lead to thanksgiving. Gratitude is the feeling; thanksgiving is the action. A lifestyle of giving thanks swallows our regrets and offers us a new way to remember.

The apostle Paul could have wallowed in regret, yet he wrote: "I do concentrate on this: I leave the past behind and with hands outstretched to whatever lies ahead I go straight for the goal—my reward the honour of being called by God in Christ."[2]

Maybe today is a good day to handle the baggage of regret one last time. To take it straight up a hill, to the foot of an old cross. To lay it down among the countless other bags left there through the centuries.

That evening after crashing my homemade time machine, I limped across our backyard and sat down beside my brother to help him examine the remains of his bicycle. "I'm…uh…glad you're alive," he said. Then a smile tugged at the corners of his lips. "The mud flaps are in excellent condition, you know. I think it was a miracle."

22

Gratitude 101

This morning my wife told me I was snoring again. I thanked her because I thought, *Here is a woman who at some point in the night made a decision to let me live.*

It is only with gratitude that life becomes rich.
DIETRICH BONHOEFFER

Each and every day I wake up and immediately take hundreds of blessings for granted. Like the fact that I woke up—and that I woke up in a bed. Spiders did not descend from the ceiling in the middle of the night as they did in a novel I just read. The ceiling did not cave in. My wife did not put a pillow over my head to halt my snoring. Ninety-five percent of humans die in their beds, I'm told. I was not one of them.

I take a breath, unaware of the miracle of such a simple act, then stagger to the bathroom, never doubting that my legs will work, that water will be there waiting for me. Clean water. Warm water. Coming from a tap.

I stumble toward the kitchen. The dog is completely out of her mind to see me but does not bite like dogs in a Stephen King film. Mine just dances in circles, drooling on me like a toddler.

In the kitchen, the fridge lights up when I open it, the coffee pot gurgles at the touch of a button, and the toaster pops up a slice of golden-brown. A table and chairs are there, along with a view. Winnie the Pooh did not visit overnight to polish off the honey. There's peanut butter too. I sit, munching away, taking for granted the fact that I can taste. Smell. See. Hear. Touch.

I say goodbye to my wife when I should be asking, "Why am I among the chosen few whose wife wants to kiss me despite morning breath and whiskers?" (Not *her* morning breath. Not her whiskers either.)

How was I singled out to spend the day engaged in meaningful work in an office free of armed guards, far from the threat of turmoil and war? Unbullied. Overfed. Appreciated.

At 5:00 p.m., I leave the office for home. Stub my toe on a door jamb. Hop in circles on one leg, holding my injured foot, squealing, "Ow, ow, ow!" Let the whining begin. A concerned friend pokes his head through my doorway and laughs. I'm the funny guy. I must be joking, right? "I'm fine," I mutter. But the truth is, I'm not. A swollen toe is just one more ailment on a growing list called "The Perils of Aging." Wrinkles on my face. Hair in my ears. Hair in my nose. Too much natural gas.

Outside, the sky is furrowed. Angry clouds move in front of the sun, and the temperature dips. My pinkie toe throbs with each stride. These new leather shoes are too tight.

When I walk through the door, my wife's Spidey sense is working. She knows within seconds how my day went. I mutter something about rainy weather and sore toes and hard shoes. I limp to the table, where steam rises from a bowl of soup next to a sandwich. I lift a spoon to my lips. The flavors dance across my palate.

Two badly needed reminders catch my gaze: a picture and a book. The picture is of a child dressed in rags, sporting a grin. My wife prays for Aldi, the child from Indonesia we sponsor through Compassion International. "Thank you, God," my wife says, "that because of your goodness to us, Aldi will go to sleep with a full belly tonight. He'll study at a school tomorrow. And learn a trade. And read a Bible. And hear about Jesus. Amen."

The book is one I was too busy to read this morning. It's still open to Psalm 23. "You prepare a table before me...you anoint my head with oil; my cup overflows. Surely goodness and mercy shall follow me all the days of my life, and I shall dwell in the house of the Lord forever" (verses 5-6 ESV).

Goodness and mercy have followed me. When did I become so adept at overlooking them? Happiness cannot be found by looking for it, but by looking elsewhere: To the needs around us, that we might meet them. To the hurts around us, that we might relieve them. To the blessings around us, that we might live in this holy moment with awe and wonder, with grace and gratitude.

So forgive me, God. Thank you for your promises, for your unmerited grace in the midst of my whining. Thanks for the 101 things I took for granted all day. For chocolate pudding and dinner with the girl who made it. For a dog who is hoping to sample it. And thank you for nine good toes.

23

Very Punny

 They're finally making a movie about clocks.
It's about time.

Friends are the siblings God never gave us.
MENCIUS

van has been my friend for almost 30 years. He loves puns. He brought me a Pop-Tart once and said, "I hear you're having a *crummy* day and you're *kneading* a lift, so I trust this will help you *rise* to the occasion. It's the *yeast* I can do." Ah, with friends like these, who needs good humor?

I took it *apun* myself to learn some puns thinking it would strengthen our friendship. But a pun is its own *re-word*. At first, I was intimidated trying to keep up with all the punning, but its *groan* on me. One day while golfing, Ivan pointed at a baby hawk high in a pine tree. "He's a *chirp* off the old block," said Ivan. I laughed. "Ah," I said, "the old bird pun. *Toucan* play at that game." When I informed Ivan that he was obsessed with puns, he said, "Don't worry. It's just a *phrase* I'm going through." Friends. What would life be without them? Without Greg dropping by with a plate of chocolate cookies. Without Kevin asking how I was doing, and sticking around for the answer. Without Harold forgiving me when I thought he wouldn't. With friends, our sorrows are halved and our joys doubled. With friends, the road is shorter and everything is funnier. Even puns.

English writer Samuel Johnson called puns "the lowest form of wit." Alfred Hitchcock called them "the highest form of literature."[1] Comedian Fred Allen said, "Hanging is too good for a man who makes puns; he should be drawn and quoted."

In fourth grade, Steve Porr told me the first pun I can remember getting. "Why are teddy bears never hungry?" I hadn't a clue. "Because they're always stuffed." The next day during science class, I got the joke and began to laugh. That was almost 50 years ago. Steve and I are still friends today.

Whether or not you enjoy puns, I think you'd agree that friends who laugh together stick together. In fact, a friend you can't laugh with is no friend at all.

Here are three physical ailments you simply must have to be a good friend.

A Sore Throat

Last winter a nagging cough blossomed into a raspy one which stole my voice and wouldn't give it back. At dinner one night, Ramona told me of her day and seemed to be enjoying herself immensely. Unable to coax out even a whisper, I scribbled on a piece of paper: "Like me better this way?" She laughed. And said, "What a blessing!"

When your throat is sore, you choose your words more carefully. You keep silent longer. You listen more. Proverbs 20:19 says, "Avoid anyone who talks too much" (NIV). Dale Carnegie wrote, "You can make more friends in two months by becoming interested in other people than you can in two years by trying to get other people interested in you."[2]

A Bad Memory

The best friends have some degree of blessed amnesia, the ability to forgive of course, but also to forget. Our best friends will disappoint—even hurt us. We can offer them a fist full of resentment or a heart full of understanding. "Bear with each other," says the writer of Colossians, "and forgive one another if any of you has a grievance against someone" (3:13-14 NIV). A bad memory helps us forget petty grievances that ruin friendships. And forgive.

Slow Reflexes

We don't jump to conclusions, fly off the handle, or race for first spot in line. We are slow to take offense, slow to get angry, slow to direct every conversation to ourselves. Philippians 2:3 says, "Do nothing from selfish ambition or conceit, but in humility count others more significant than yourselves" (ESV). We emphasize *their* strengths, *their* virtues. We mention our faults and foibles before criticizing theirs.

A sore throat. A bad memory. Slow reflexes. Three starting points to being the kind of friend we'd like to have as a friend—one who laughs, even when our jokes are corny. Which reminds me of the time Ivan stopped by to tell me that another friend of his was crushed by a pile of books.

I said, "That's terrible."

He said, "Yes, but he's only got his *shelf* to blame."

24

Makin' Carrot Biscuits

 When I turned fifty, I looked in the mirror. I said to my wife, "I don't look fifty." She said, "No, but you used to."

More marriages might survive if the partners realized that sometimes the better comes after the worse.

DOUG LARSON

Did you ever hear a song and think it said something it didn't? In eighth grade I heard Randy Bachman belt out the song "Takin' Care of Business," and a friend told me what he thought it said. I walked around for a week singing, "Makin' carrot biscuits." I still sing it that way.

A year or two later, my older brothers began sneaking Bee Gees vinyl records into the house and playing them at 4,000 decibels when my parents were out at prayer meetings. The Bee Gees were undeniably talented, but approximately 23 percent of their lyrics are indecipherable. Is the song "Stayin' Alive" or "Stay in the Line"? It's hard to tell. "More Than a Woman" kind of sounds like "Bald-Headed Woman" to me.

The Bee Gees weren't alone in the pop world. My friend Vance hears the song "Can't Fight This Feeling" by REO Speedwagon and sings, "Can't climb this ceiling."

The term for this is *mondegreen*. It's "a word or phrase that results from a mishearing of something said or sung."[1] So when Steve Winwood sings the song "Higher Love," and you think it's "Pie of Love," you've created another mondegreen.

The American writer Sylvia Wright coined the word in 1954. As a young girl, she misinterpreted a line from an old Scottish poem, "They hae slain the Earl o' Moray and laid him on the green," thinking the last part said, "Lady Mondegreen."[2] *Voilà*, a new word was born.

One morning in church a father leaned toward his son to see if he was hearing correctly. Sure enough. While the rest were singing, "The King is Exalted," the little guy was singing with sincerity, "The King is Exhausted."

Here are other memorable lines smiling parents have heard.

"He's trampling out the vintage where the great giraffe is stored."[3]

"Behold he comes, riding on a cow."[4]

"I Got Peas In My Liver."[5]

"I am a friend of God, he calls me Fred."[6]

Yvonne's toddler lifted his hands like he saw Daddy doing and sang, "Open the Eyes of My Hot Dog."[7]

Heidi's five-year-old said, "Mom, let's sing 'The Zombie Song.'"[8] "The what?" Mom asked. "You know…Jesus wants me for a zombie!"

A little girl asked her mom, "Why does God think we are salty?" Her mom asked what she meant, so the girl sang, "I am salty…" Of course the real words are, "I exalt thee."

Even the Psalms can be misheard. A boy had been learning Psalm 23 at Sunday School. Later his mom heard him muttering, "Surely good Miss Murphy shall follow me all the days of my life."

Unlike the Bee Gees, God never mumbles. He is crystal clear on things that really matter. Mark Twain was credited with saying, "It ain't those parts of the Bible I don't understand that bother me; it's the parts that I do understand."

One night I read in Ephesians 5, "Husbands, love your wives, as Christ loved the church" (verse 25 ESV). I remember thinking, *But the spark is gone. I'm not in love anymore. In fact, I don't even like her.* And though God has never physically taken hold of me by the ears and pushed me against the wall, he came real close that day. As clearly as I've heard anything in my life, I heard him say, "Callaway, I never told you to like her. I never told you to feel warm fuzzies. I told you to love her. To be kind. Tender-hearted. Forgiving. Just as I've forgiven you."

My wife tells a similar story about reading that same chapter. She read the words, "The wife must respect her husband" (verse 33 NIV), knowing she was struggling to do so at the time. And she thought to herself, *How do I respect him when I don't respect him?* God clearly spoke to her: "Work at it. Do it." And so she did. She began to find ways to look past my ample faults and see strengths to encourage. That changed our marriage. I suppose it helped that there was also an abrupt change in me. One night, I rolled up my sleeves and did the dishes. She's still in shock.

As we did the dishes, she began to sing the Beatles song "All My Loving." I sang along. But I sang "All my luggage." We laughed together. It was a miracle—as any lasting marriage is.

25

Spite House

 Did you ever throw out a picture your child painted then think, *Oh no! What if she becomes the next great artist? I'll have thrown out about a billion dollars' worth of paintings!*

When the root is bitterness, imagine
what the fruit might be.
WOODROW KROLL

Some think millionaires live without problems. But Joseph Richardson had one. The wealthy New York contractor owned an unusual ribbon of land—a hundred feet long and just a couple yards wide. No one had invented water slides as of yet, so he approached his neighbor, wealthy clothier Hyman Sarner. Would he purchase the lot for $5,000?

Sarner never complained about the noise when opportunity knocked. He listened. And hatched a plan. He would add the land to his adjoining land and build an apartment complex. "I really have no use for it," he said, "but you can't build on it. So I'll take it off your hands as a favor. I'll give you a thousand dollars."

Richardson blew a gasket. "You tightwad," he yelled. "That's one-tenth of what it's worth. I'll show you." As the door slammed in his face, an idea formed in his head. So it was that in 1882, Richardson built a gaping eyesore of a house that ran the full length of his property and was just five feet wide. Filled with tiny rooms, the house was barely able to hold a stick of furniture. Passersby talked and gawked. Neighbors complained. Richardson cared not a smidgen. He moved into his uncomfortable house, condemning himself to a prison of revenge. There he remained until his death.

They are called "spite houses." Monuments to hate. Legend says that Boston's narrowest was built when two brothers inherited land. While one was away in the military, the other built a large home for himself on the land. Upon returning, his soldier brother erected a tiny spite house to block out sunlight and spoil his brother's view of the nearby waterway.

It seems unthinkable. But most of us have been chained by bitterness, imprisoned in the house that spite built. It may involve a business deal, a former spouse, or a once-trusted friend. Sure, we know we must move on. But the memories swirl, stoking regret, swiping our joy, and leaving us in a prison every bit as real as that tiny spite house.

We know what God asks of us: "Get rid of all bitterness, rage, anger, harsh words, and slander…Instead, be kind to each other, tenderhearted, forgiving one another, just as God through Christ has forgiven you" (Ephesians 4:31-32).

But how is that possible?

I once spoke at a center for women recovering from addiction. Most had been horribly abused. On the way there I asked Ramona, "What could I possibly say to these ladies?"

She said, "Tell them about your mom."

So that afternoon we sat around a table as I told these precious children of God my mother's story, of the years of abuse. Of how she took the very thing that could have defined her and turned it upside down. How on Tuesdays women came to our home for supper, then sat in the living room where I sometimes heard them laughing, then crying. I didn't know for decades of the transformation taking place. But after Mom's funeral, handwritten letters arrived. Three were from best-selling authors essentially saying the same thing: "I wouldn't have written a paragraph without those Tuesday nights." They needed the hope a fellow struggler provided. One who had been there. "It's God's grace," Mom told me over and over when her depression lifted. "God's grace alone."

Those words returned to me after a business associate broke promises and made loud threats. Like all great geysers, he spouted off regularly. But there was no humor in it. I lay awake, tortured by acid-injected memories that raced through my mind. Self-pity. Resentment. Rage. It's a bitter cycle. The cure was months in coming. It arrived only when I learned a secret my mother told me about.

Peace comes when I shift my focus from what has been done *to* me to what has been done *for* me.

Such a shift starts with gratitude and continues by God's grace.

My dad was part Scotch and part club soda until Jesus got hold of him and he experienced that amazing grace. He loved few things more than a good story, like this one:

In a Scottish seaside inn, the fishermen were boasting. One put his hands out so wide to describe a fish he'd caught that he sent a teapot crashing against the wall. The innkeeper was shocked when he saw the ugly brown stain. "It'll never come out," he said.

A stranger at a corner table stepped forward. "Perhaps not," he said. "But if my work meets your approval, you won't need to repaint."

The stranger removed brushes and paint from a box. He then sketched lines around the stain. Dabbed bits of color here and there.

Turned the splotches of tea into the image of a deer with a magnificent set of antlers. At the bottom, he inscribed his signature, paid his bill, and left.

The innkeeper stepped forward and squinted at the signature. The man was the much-loved wildlife painter, E.H. Landseer. The ugly stain had been transformed for all to see.

For now, you may wonder how it is possible for God to transform your pain and hurt. But it's what he does. That's his business. Ours is to bid bitterness goodbye. Is it easy? Are you kidding? It just may be the hardest test of our lives. But we must focus not on what has been done *to* us, but on what God's Son, Jesus, has done *for* us on the cross. He alone can remove those bitter stains and transform us for good.

26

"New" Steps to Happiness

 I dropped my phone from a fourteenth-floor window. Thank goodness for "airplane mode."

Affection is responsible for nine-tenths of whatever solid and durable happiness there is in our natural lives.

C.S. LEWIS

There are three certainties in life: death, taxes, and the fact that one day you will gaze into a drawer and think, *Where did all these pens come from?*

Another certainty is that somewhere, right now, someone is happily counting money they have received from a government grant to study happiness. *Time* magazine's article "New Ways to Become Happier—and Healthier"[1] is one such study. According to the article, there are "science-backed tips" you need to know in order to "find more joy in your life." Here are just three:

Explore life without social media.

If you want to be happier, start here. As the article notes, social media now dictates how a majority of us navigate our daily lives and interact with friends and strangers. But the constant negative exposure from the moment we awake until we drift off, scientists say, is taking its toll on our level of happiness. New studies are linking frequent social media use with poorer mental and physical health and increased anxiety. The influx of disturbing headlines and upsetting opinions steals joy faster than a teenager can gobble your pizza.

Tristan Harris, a former product manager at Google, accuses the big platforms of "hijacking our minds."[2] He explains how Apple, Facebook, Google, Twitter, Snapchat, and others manipulate our attention to keep us hooked to our screen for as long and as frequently as possible. In the meantime, recent research shows that the mere presence of one's smartphone reduces available cognitive capacity.[3] I find it fascinating that executives who have worked hard to fill classrooms with computers are sending their own children to schools that use actual pens, paper, and knitting needles so their kids can engage in physical activity and hands-on learning.[4]

What do researchers advise? Trim your social networking habit. Take a break. Get outside. Do something. Anything! People who quit Facebook for just a week experienced major leaps in life satisfaction. And the more a person used Facebook before taking a break, the greater their happiness after giving it up.[5]

Deploy random acts of kindness.

Doing a favor for your spouse, scientists claim, can boost your emotional well-being, even if—get this—they don't thank you for it. Psychologists asked 175 newlyweds to jot down times when their spouse set aside personal wishes in order to meet their partner's needs, such as sweeping the floor or doing the dishes. Acts of kindness made both of them happier, whether or not the action was acknowledged. And the one who performed the selfless act received greater satisfaction than the recipient. Historically, we have referred to this as "servanthood."

Humans are wired to give, claims the *Time* study. In fact, researchers even conclude that giving money boosts happiness, but only when the goal is to benefit the receiver, not to impress them with generosity or to get something in return. Which leads me to believe that readers who send me chocolate bars would experience greater happiness. (I'm just trying to be helpful, of course.)

Let go of grudges.

Those who are more stressed have worse mental and physical health. But forgiving both yourself and others can protect against stress and the toll it takes on your mental health. In fact, being quick to forgive erases the connection between stress and mental illness. If you don't forgive, says the study, you don't have a buffer against stress. And I like this: "Research has shown that saying a short prayer…can help people take the edge off."[6]

Isn't it fascinating—and just a tad bit humorous—that we spend money to discover "new ways" that are already found in the "book of joy," which is what I call the book of Philippians? Without a doubt it is the happiest book in the Bible. We find these three happiness points covered there, along with a hundred others.

Though Greek scholars believe iPhones aren't mentioned directly, Paul invites us to think on things that are true, noble, right, pure, lovely, admirable, and praiseworthy (Philippians 4:8). We may find these virtues on social media, but there are better places to go looking.

Paul also applauds acts of kindness, saying, "Let everyone see that you are considerate in all you do" (4:5) and, "Don't look out only for your own interests, but take an interest in others, too" (2:4). If this attitude characterized our days, I doubt we'd be looking for new ways to be happier and healthier.

Paul also models grudgeless living. After being beaten, maligned, and imprisoned, he writes words that have not a hint of bitterness but are jam-packed with joy: "Rejoice in the Lord always. I will say it again: Rejoice!" (4:4 NIV). Paul didn't learn this from the latest study, but from Jesus, who taught his followers to love our enemies and forgive our debtors. In Jesus' last moments leading up to his death, he prayed for those who tormented him: "Father, forgive them, for they know not what they do" (Luke 23:34 ESV).

Some call it a "new" way; I call it tried and true. Laughing like a kid again just may be easier than we think when we ignore our phones a little more, spread some kindness around, and lay down whatever grudges we've picked up along the way.

27

Lettuce Theology

 Ever been on hold for so long that you can't remember who you called? "Uh, yes, hello…who are you? What do you do again?"

Me: "Who loves you?"

Sophie (age 3): "Bumpa."

Me: "Who would climb that maple tree for you?"

Sophie: "Bumpa."

Me: "Who would go to the moon and back for you?"

Sophie: "Jesus."

hope you have a hobby. I have two: playing golf and growing veggies. For some, these activities sound about as exciting as watching cheese mold, but I find them therapeutic. Without a doubt golf is the more maddening of the two. A golf pro has tried to help but keeps threatening to give up the game because of me. My green-thumbed wife is the garden pro, and she's helping me learn gardening. "Perseverance worketh patience," my father liked to say. And patience is something I'm helping my wife learn.

Just before lunch one warm Saturday in June, my wife was off with a friend for a walk. Since we'd had a low-grade disagreement

that morning, I thought, *Hey. I'll do something nice. I'll surprise her.*
I did the standard guy stuff. Snipped the grass. Nipped the hedge.
Then I even yanked a few weeds from her flower garden. I have no
idea what came over me. I'm just reporting the facts.

Now, Ramona's flower garden is enviable and magnificent. People stop by just to gaze and comment—which is why I was so surprised to find a weed in it. A sizable weed which had somehow gone
unnoticed and taken up residence. It's one of those daisy look-alikes.
An impostor. A phony. These little fraudsters spread their noxious
seeds and strangle other plants if you're not careful. You've got to
stay on top of them. Vigilance is the key.

So I pulled on the cluster. The stupid thing wouldn't budge. I
got a shovel and hacked around it until the pretender relented and
came out by the roots. Not wanting any seeds to spread, I carefully
wrapped it in a trash bag, plunked it on the curb, and smiled. Boy,
did my wife hit the jackpot with me.

An hour later, I saw her standing by her immaculately groomed
flower garden, shaking her head. "See that hole?" I said. "There was
a weed right there." I pointed. "I killed the stupid thing."

"Weed?" She was holding her forehead now and repeating herself. "Weed? That was no weed. That was common yarrow. *Achil-
lea millefolium.*"

"Oh," I said. "Crud."

"It was not crud," she said. "It was very nice."

"I'm sorry." I half expected her to scream. She had every reason. After all, I had murdered her *Achilles heelafolium.* Instead, she
raised her eyebrows at me, removed the hand from her forehead,
bent over a bit, and started to laugh. I thank God for that laugh. It
is the kind of laugh uttered by a patient, long-suffering, and self-
controlled woman. It is nurtured by kindness, gentleness, faith, and
meekness, which—when blended together—serve to lavish love, joy,
and peace upon a home. The Bible calls them "fruits of the Spirit."[1]

My misdiagnosis in the flower garden got me thinking—work

with me here—of the "veggies of the Spirit." Call it "lettuce theology," if you will. My wife says there are five classifications of lettuce: looseleaf, romaine, celtuce, butterhead, and crisphead—words my brothers called me. By my count, there are about 145 uses of "let us" in the Bible.

Here is my top-ten "Let Us" list. Tossed together, they offer us a splendid recipe.

Joy Salad

1. "Let us follow the Spirit's leading in every part of our lives" (Galatians 5:25).

2. "Let us aim for harmony in the church and try to build each other up" (Romans 14:19).

3. "If we have enough food and clothing, let us be content" (1 Timothy 6:8).

4. "Let us cleanse ourselves from everything that can defile our body or spirit" (2 Corinthians 7:1).

5. "Let us not become conceited, or provoke one another, or be jealous of one another" (Galatians 5:26).

6. "Let us hold firmly to what we believe" (Hebrews 4:14).

7. "Let us come boldly to the throne of our gracious God. There we will receive his mercy, and we will find grace to help us when we need it most" (Hebrews 4:16).

8. "Let us hold tightly without wavering to the hope we affirm, for God can be trusted to keep his promise" (Hebrews 10:23).

9. "Let us run with endurance the race God has set before us" (Hebrews 12:1).

10. "Since we are receiving a Kingdom that is unshakable, let us be thankful" (Hebrews 12:28).

I plan on reading this list to my wife. She's out for another walk. I think I'll clean the closet while she's gone. Maybe throw out some of her old pairs of shoes.

28

Seven Coincidences

 I had a high school teacher who said that all of us descended from monkeys and apes, but it shows up more on some people.

Truth is not a chameleon that changes its political colors with each generation in the hope of reelection. It is what it is, like it or not.

ALICIA BRITT CHOLE

Have you ever witnessed a coincidence? Recently I found myself hours from home on a stage being introduced by a guy who was wearing the same brand and color of shirt I was wearing. The sizes were even the same.

That's nothing compared to the seven crazy coincidences below.

A four-year-old Colorado boy fell out of a third-floor window, did two summersaults, and landed on his feet. "I fall…really, really far," the boy said. His mother said she was "beyond lucky." He also happened to be wearing a Superman shirt.[1]

According to *The Blunder Book*, in 1895 there were only two cars in the state of Ohio. Sadly, they managed to run into each other.

Hitler came to power 129 years after Napoleon crowned himself Emperor, invaded Russia 129 years after Napoleon did the same, and was defeated in Paris in 1944, 129 years after Napoleon was finally defeated.

Violet Jessop, an Argentine ocean liner stewardess and nurse, was known as "Miss Unsinkable." She was aboard the RMS *Olympic* in 1911 when it struck the HMS *Hawke*, the HMHS *Britannic* in 1916 when it hit a mine, and the RMS *Titanic* when it struck ice and sunk in 1912. Violet lived to be 83.

During the 1930s, a man named Joseph Figlock was out for a walk when a baby fell out of a window, landing on Joseph's shoulders. One year later, another baby fell out of another window onto Joseph again. No word as to what was going on in the poor children's houses.

Less than a year before John Wilkes Booth killed Abraham Lincoln, Booth's brother Edwin saved the life of Lincoln's eldest son, Robert.

Around 1940, twin boys were separated not long after their birth. Their adopting families named them both Jim. Both men married a woman named Linda (not the same woman, I presume) and then later got remarried to a woman named Betty. Both had a son they named James Alan (one spelled the middle name *Allan*). Both had a dog named Toy. In 1979, the men were reunited. Imagine their laughter upon discovering these and other amazing coincidences.

At times a remarkable concurrence of events can happen. But we can't stake our lives on it. Recently I asked a 25-year-old who had been searching for God, "When you look at the night sky, do you think all this is coincidence?"

She smiled. "Impossible," she said. "My parents and teachers taught me that. But I don't buy it. How could this all have just happened?"

Author and scientist Francis Collins said in an interview, "When you look from the perspective of a scientist at the universe, it looks as if it knew we were coming. There are 15 constants—the gravitational constant, various constants about the strong and weak nuclear force, and the like—that have precise values. If any one of those constants was off by even one part in a million, or in some cases, by one part in a million million, the universe could not have actually come to the point where we see it…There would have been no galaxy, stars, planets or people."[2]

So here we are.

None of the seven whopping coincidences I've mentioned come within a billion light years of the notion that nothing could come from nothing.

It is my prayer that you will never face the ultimate regret of placing your faith in something that is unsustainable. Instead, simply acknowledge that the complexity and beauty of the universe shout, "Hey! There is a God. A God who cares. A God who is knowable. A God who is joy itself."

After growing up a confirmed atheist, Alicia Britt Chole delivered the salutatorian address at her high school graduation. Among her words were these: "Let's see in ten years at our class reunion if the class…fulfilled the potential we all know we have." Exactly ten years later, she found herself back in Weslaco, Texas, with her classmates. A friend recounts what happened.

> I asked Alicia to say the prayer before dinner…I knew it would totally freak people out. I knew Alicia had changed, but my classmates didn't know…They remember Alicia as she was…an atheist. The most incredible thing to me was they didn't even recognize Alicia. Alicia's countenance had changed. The hardness was gone and now there was peace. She had a glow about her.[3]

She had fulfilled her potential.

Does faith require us to switch off our brains, live in denial, and chuck our questions overboard? No. But as Alicia puts it, "Believing does mean that you can know the living God."[4]

Walking with God, she later says, sharpened, not dulled, her mind. It broadened, not narrowed, her base of knowledge and experience. On a hurting planet, where joy and pain coexist, she came to see God as the ultimate realist. "God does not conveniently edit out the uncomfortable," she wrote.[5]

We all have faith. But to place it in coincidence—believing that all this stunning, fine-tuned beauty did not come from a designer—seems akin to believing I could whack 6 million consecutive 95-mile-an-hour fastballs over the center field fence into the same guy's drink while batting left-handed.

After an event, a little boy came up to me and told me a joke. "Did you know that baseball is mentioned in the Bible?" I told him I did not. He said, "In the big inning…"

Well, "In the beginning," the book of Genesis tells us, "God created the heavens and the earth" (1:1 NIV). Nothing else comes close to making any plausible sense to me. No one but our creator holds the manual for living with purpose and meaning—and, in the end, without regrets.

Part 3

Leave Footsteps Worth Following

 A little kid asked his grandpa, "What if a policeman lied and turned on his siren but he was just going to get a taco for lunch?"

'm from a small town. How small? The last one to bed turns out the streetlight. A night on the town takes about four minutes—unless you run into someone you know (which is everyone). As a child I couldn't get away with a thing. I cussed, and my parents knew about it in four minutes.

I travel far but still live in the same town, because where else can you find the entertainment a small town newspaper provides? "Police received report of suspicious behavior. Turned out to be three males with flashlights comparing facial hair." One week no one died, so the obituary section just said, "Deaths are coming."

Whenever I return home from the international airport an hour away from town, I drive past our cemetery, the college where I studied, the high school that issued my first diploma, the elementary school where I honed my humor, and the playground where I spent half my childhood falling off monkey bars. I leave town, and the order reverses. Life flashes before me. It takes maybe two minutes.

"Teach us how short our lives really are," wrote the psalmist, "so that we may be wise."[1] Wherever we live, we're not here long. "Deaths are coming." Each day matters. We all leave footsteps. By God's grace, they can be footsteps worth following.

The godly walk with integrity;
blessed are their children who follow them.

PROVERBS 20:7

29

The Nicest Thing Ever Said

 I was thinking, *Wouldn't it be great if my dog could talk?* And then I thought, *Are you kidding? I've said some really dumb things to my dog. What if he told people?*

You can't always stop people from being mean.
But you can stop them from making you mean.
MIKE MASON

Years ago, when I should have known better, I bought a book about put-downs. In my defense, it was severely discounted, and I couldn't bring myself to turn my back on such a bargain. My Scottish ancestors would be proud.

Within this book's pages was an astonishing array of clever comebacks and witty one-liners. A quick flip through the book was enjoyable, but I didn't get far without wincing. Humorists like me live inches away from severing relationships, employing our tongues as pitchforks, dissecting bosses or pastors or the next generation, and sucking the joy from a room like a skunk at a perfume convention.

It seems we live in mean times, when the ugly goo of pent-up anger and cynicism is bubbling over the top of the cauldron. But those who leave footsteps worth following are writing a book about buildups rather than put-downs.

Recently, I began asking friends to write down the nicest thing someone ever said to them. I was surprised how the question made them smile and how quickly the answers came. Most were short and sweet, like...

- "I forgive you."

- "I love you."

- "You're funny."

- "Thanks."

- "I'm proud of you."

- "You changed my life."

- "You're a great mother-in-law."

- "You're a breath of fresh air."

- "Yes."

A few made me smile too.

Alfie White told me, "After a nurse flushed my ears, she said, 'You have the nicest ear canals I've ever seen.'"

Someone told Ed Wallan he looked a lot like Clark Gable. "I was flattered," said Ed, "until I realized that Clark had been dead for 50 years."

Kim Turner lives one door north of us. Her life changed when someone asked her mom, "May I take her to Sunday school? I think she'll like it." Kim's mother said yes. Kim says, "I went to Sunday school and slowly began my walk with Jesus. That single invitation changed the course of my life."

One time Shawn Brama was traveling long-distance by Greyhound bus with her active children, aged two and three. Her eyeglasses had snapped in half, blurring everything beyond three feet. So she read the kids story after story as others slept. When her energetic three-year-old bounced up and down, she sang a song about a teddy bear to soothe him.

"When we finally reached our destination," she remembers, "I knew everyone had been staring at us. As we exited the bus, an older lady smiled and said, 'You are such a wonderful mother.' Those words made my day. I've never forgotten how much they encouraged me. I pass them along to other parents often."

Arriving in a swimming pool changing room, my wife heard a lady singing a beautiful worship song. Ramona said, "Sing it, sister!"

The lady stopped. "Oh, I'm sorry. I'm embarrassed. I didn't know anyone was here."

Ramona said, "You sing beautifully. You should sing more often."

The lady smiled. "My mother sometimes told me not to sing. She didn't like my voice."

"I like it," said Ramona, smiling, "and I've got good taste in music."

Words are like salt. When blurted unwisely they bring sickness, burden the heart, and increase blood pressure. When sprinkled rightly they add flavor, preserve life, and melt ice. It is impossible to overestimate the importance of using our words to build up. Gossip tears down. But when we live by the rule that others are safe in the room when they're not present, we will exceed our legal limit in friends.

I cannot tell you who won the World Series three years ago. Or the Grand Prix. Or the Tour de France. But I can tell you exactly where I was standing when Cordell Darling said, "If you ever write a book, I'll buy a dozen." His words gave me enough motivation and encouragement to write my first dozen.

I cannot tell you much about my fifth year of life, but I remember the night my mom tucked me into bed and said, "I'll miss you while you're sleeping." She may have been fudging the truth a little, but like no one else I've known, she modeled the fine art of encouragement.

I cannot list for you the top five pitchers or hockey players, but I can tell you the color of my dad's shirt the first time he said, "I love you." Dad was 75. I never doubted that he loved me. But it sure was nice hearing those words.

I have yet to meet a successful, influential person who couldn't point to a time in their life when simple words of encouragement changed them.

Ephesians 4:29 says, "Watch the way you talk...Say only what helps, each word a gift" (MSG). A few simple, life-giving words can alter the trajectory of someone's life.

And what is the nicest thing someone ever said to me? It may sound sappy, but it's true: My wife said, "I do." And she did.

30

Daddy of the Bride

Here's a little advice for you guys out there. I know you would never forget your wife's birthday. But if you did—and let me say once again that you wouldn't—but if it were to happen, here's what to say: "How can I remember your birthday when you never look any older?"

Annie: I couldn't sleep. I just kept thinking about how this was my last night in my bed...in my house... kinda like my last night as a kid. I mean, I've lived here since I was five and I feel like I'm supposed to turn in my key tomorrow....I mean, I know I can't stay, but it's like I don't want to leave.

George: Well, that's the thing about life...is uh, the surprises. The little things that sneak up on you and grab hold of you. Still happens to me.

STEVE MARTIN AND KIMBERLY WILLIAMS-PAISLEY IN *FATHER OF THE BRIDE*

There's no real job description for the father of the bride. You stand around faking patience and bravery, telling fibs like, "I'd love to buy that dress for you," and, "Sure, go ahead. No problem. I'll just write a check." And all the while you have as much control of your emotions as a Brazilian soccer fan. You smile when it makes no sense, choke back unsolicited advice, and barricade the tears when she says, "Let's go for one last walk. Tomorrow I change my name."

The unimpeachable truth is she's had you wrapped around her pinkie for 22 years. And when this stunningly gorgeous gal takes your arm and pulls you down the aisle, the minister talks, but you don't hear him. You're too busy staring daggers at the boy you've been trying to keep on curfew for months.

"Does anyone have a reason these two should not be joined?"

"Me. I have three hundred reasons."

But you choose the right to remain silent and sit beside your wife, who is dabbing her eyes with a beach towel. "I'll tell you why people cry at weddings," you say. "They haven't slept for three days."

Rachael stands there looking like an opportunity missed by Rembrandt, and I start dabbing my eyes, too, as she says, "Jordan Matthew, I promise to put Jesus first in our marriage, to love him more than I love you, for only then can I truly show you love. I promise to make you laugh often and to be faithful. To make home a place you run to and want to stay. I will care for you, be your help-mate, encourage you, and stand by you no matter what. I give my heart to you, to guard and protect. I love you."

Behind us sits my brother-in-law Bill. Thirty-four years ago today he vowed to be true to my wife's sister. And then Hunting-ton's disease arrived, and the slow ride to the nursing home began. For 25 years he nursed his bride. "In sickness and in health," the minister says. I live surrounded by heroes. Men and women who cemented these vows years ago.

Perhaps that's why my voice quivers at the reception, and I'm thankful for notes. "My darling Rachael: You've been an absolute delight to have as a daughter. Except for that day when you called and said, 'Dad, I have great news. Your airbags work just fine.'

"We've been praying for this day for twenty-two years, Rachael. Not because we wanted to get rid of you, but because we wanted to see you hanging on to a guy who is head-over-boots in love with you. Someone said, 'Don't think of it so much as losing a daughter.' They're right. I think of it as *paying* to lose a daughter. You're worth every penny. Sadly, no one takes pennies. They want twenties and hundreds.

"When you were small, I tucked you in with butterfly kisses. A nose rub. Fluttering eyelashes. 'I love you, Rachael.' 'Love you too, Daddy,' you always said. Remember, Jordan, I loved her first.

"Your friend Simone asked if I was gonna cry walking you down the aisle. I told her if I did it would be because I was about to hand the *Mona Lisa* to a three-hundred-pound orangutan. She laughed because she knows that Jordan is anything but. He's only two hundred pounds. Seriously, we love you, Jordan.

"Thanks to you both for waiting. Like you, Mom and I didn't share a pillow until our wedding night. We've had regrets. That's not one of them. Years ago, we memorized Psalm 48:14: 'This God is our God for ever and ever: he will be our guide even unto death.'[1] He's been there all the way.

"We thank God for you both. We'll be cheering and praying. And the fridge will always be stocked. Though I'll be putting a lock on it now.

"Grandpa and Grandma would have loved to see this day. They passed along so many great family traditions. For instance, they went along on all their kids' honeymoons. We can't wait to spend the next two weeks with you in Turtle Lake, Montana.

"And to all my friends about to partake in this six-course meal, I want you to know that we are enrolled in the gift registry at First National Bank."

31

Letter to Judah

 We have grandkids now, and I just realized that
you see much more of your children after they
leave home.

If nothing is going well, call your grandmother.

ITALIAN PROVERB

Dear Judah Matthew,

I'm your grandpa. The one who said to your parents, "Have kids while we're still young enough to take care of them for you." I'm the guy who stubbed his toe on a chair, then just about drove over a cat speeding to the hospital to see you. I was that excited. And here you are, my very first grandson—all seven pounds, thirteen ounces of you.

Allow me to warn you of a few things, Judah. First off, you have an older sister and two cousins. All girls. Girls are fine, but you must learn to stand up to them. They will dress you in doll clothes, slop mascara on your eyelids, and put curlers in your hair. Smile. You'll be okay. You won't be able to talk for yourself for a while, so I will say something to them.

I love having granddaughters, but they are cunning and ingenious, and they're not even two yet. They bat their eyelids, and I will do anything they ask. I am putty in their hands. But I will not be putty with you. No, sir. You are a boy. I shall paw the ground and snort at you. And after that, well, I will likely fetch you anything you want.

I quite like being a grandpa. It's God's compensation plan for growing old. And the job description is shorter than a toddler's pool cue.

- Carry Gummi Bears—gluten-free, sugar-free, fat-free.

- Have time.

- Say yes a lot.

- Slow down around bugs and caterpillars and dirt.

- Fix stuff.

- Love unconditionally.

- Model goofiness.

- Model godliness.

- If you set a grandchild down, don't forget where you left them.

Other than that, there isn't much to it.

A word of warning about your parents. They are still pretty new at this parenting thing, so cut them some slack. Especially your dad. If he falls asleep while changing your diaper, he has had a long day. Be patient. It is a virtue best developed early. As for your mom: She's my little girl. Be very nice to her. She will choose your meals for the next 18 years.

Now, a word about your names: Judah and Matthew. You were christened after a scoundrel and a tax collector.

Bible names from perfect people are hard to find.

Matthew was the tax collector. He liked other people's money.

He had people fill out forms. "How much money did you make last year? Send it in."

Judah was a type A scoundrel. I read about him when I was a teen. How God allowed him in the Bible at all mystified me.

But here's the deal. These are the people God loves and calls and forgives and changes and uses. You, my child, are a marvelous reminder of God's much-needed grace in my own life. Of his ability to mend the busted and bring hope to the hopeless. I give thanks each day for that grace, because I've been a scoundrel too. I've needed forgiveness. Just ask your grandma. On second thought, don't. She might tell you.

A warning about the planet you landed on: Things are pretty dark here. We have an enemy, and he's not a fan of light. He likes to take everything that's pure and make it ugly. But God takes what's busted and makes it beautiful. Never forget, God is greater than any obstacle you will face.

Last night we committed you to God. He has awesome plans for you, Judah Matthew. I'm so glad he included me in that plan. We prayed for you, then I held you very close and whispered, "I will saw off a golf club for you. Maybe we can get out to the course together next week."

You opened one eye, and I think you may have winked at me. Or perhaps you had gas.

You have made me a very happy guy, Judah. And you've yet to say a word. I can't wait to teach you how to whistle with a blade of grass, make faces with a flashlight, tie a necktie, tell a joke, throw a curveball, treat a lady well, and spin in circles until you can't stand up. But first it's time for your father to change your diaper. Then I'll show you what a Gummi Bear looks like. And take these curlers out of your hair.

Your friend for always, Grandpa Phil

Photos and flu bugs: Photos with the eight grandkids are a hoot. Most are of blurry heads and backsides and flailing arms and fingers in nostrils. This was the best we could muster with flu bugs flying. (Left to right: Aaron, Judah, Seth, Caleb, Eowyn, Macy, Claira, and 101-degree Sophia.)

32

The Proverbs 31 Dad

> My dad used to let me ride on his shoulders. But one time he warned me. He said, "Hey, you keep pulling my hair, you'll have to get down." I said, "But I'm just trying to get my gum back!"

While it is well enough to leave footprints on the sands of time, it is even more important to make sure they point in a commendable direction.

JAMES BRANCH CABELL

'm told there are more phone calls placed on Mother's Day than on any other holiday. Back in the days of *collect* phone calls (where the person called does the paying), there were more placed on Father's Day than any other day of the year.[1]

One reason I called my dad collect when I got older is that he cut my hair when I was small. Dad had a finely honed barbering technique. He would start on one side of my head and cut for a while. Then he would amble around to the other side, and—relying on memory—try to even it up. This never worked out in my favor. In fact, it left me with about 34 jagged hairs on my shiny little head.

When I was four or five, my mother first uttered the immortal words, "You just wait 'til your father gets home." It's the first time

I remember living in mortal fear of my dad. I paced the house for seven hours. Thank goodness Mom was a good forgetter. Forgetfulness in a parent is the gift that keeps on giving. But one of the greatest gifts my dad gave me came along because he was worried about me.

As the youngest in the family, I had to come up with creative ways to get noticed. My siblings were featured prominently in photo albums. I was not. In fact, to this day I think there are maybe two photos of me somewhere. In both I'm way off in the background, a little fuzzy, yelling, "Hey, it's me! Over here!"

One day while working hard to gain attention, I made a remarkable discovery. Swear words did the trick. I never employed them around my parents, but word travels fast in a small town. I didn't have to wait long for my father to come home that day. He found me quickly. And we had a little chat. He even brought a King James Bible with him. But he didn't preach. Simply smiled and told me how God got hold of his tongue when he was a teenager. Then he offered me a watch if I would read a chapter from the book of Proverbs each day for a month. That was it. He never repeated the offer.

That night I began to discover 31 surprisingly frank chapters packed with timeless wisdom. Many tell men to smarten up and guard our hearts and minds. The final chapter is a beautiful—and at times intimidating—ode to mothers. The book prepared me for Mother's and Father's Day sermons in our church, I suppose. Moms were praised there. Fathers, well, not so much.

My dad lived a dozen miles from perfect, yet I often reflect on the things he did well. The watch is gone. So is Dad. I can't ask him for money or a haircut or call him collect. But I miss him every day. And I thought of him as I wrote a little poem loosely adapted from that glorious ode to the perfect wife and mother that I first read when I was 12.

This is my take on the Proverbs 31 dad:

A good husband is hard to find,
    and worth more than a lifetime supply of Belgian chocolate.
His wife trusteth him without regret,
    enjoying his company so much that she may even golf with
    him,
        should she take leave of her senses.
He buyeth her the choicest of finery,
    but never on credit.
He payeth more attention to his children
    than his smartphone or Netflix.
Somehow he findeth time to attend some of their sporting events,
    stifling his desire to scream at referees.
He doth also attend the odd recital, never wincing
    nor bursting forth with laughter
        when sour trumpet notes are hit.
He naggeth not his children,
    loving the sound of their laughter
        more than that of ESPN Radio.
Though screaming ensues, he dealeth with it calmly,
    disciplining in love, then buying ice cream.
He kisseth owies, repaireth leaky sinks and shattered vases,
    muttering but softly when he stubbeth his toe.
He praiseth his wife for hard work and new hairdos,
    and provideth gladly for his family.
He prefereth a home to a house,
    a car that's paid for to the smell of new leather seats.

Selah.

With great wisdom doth he bring along a book to read,
    while his wife shoppeth for clothes.
He forgetteth not his anniversary,
    and complimenteth his wife's fashionability—yea, even her
    purse.
With gladness doth he make the bed—
    on her seventy-eighth birthday.

He complaineth not about the in-laws,
 but joyfully cutteth the roast whilst they visit.
He careth more about widows and orphans
 than buying boats and vacation homes.
He chooseth wisely his online friends,
 avoiding the second glance
 and the seedy side of the internet.
He keepeth his word, even when it hurts.
He doeth the right thing, even when no one is there
 to appreciate it.
Though his girth may resurge and his hairline recede,
 he laughs at the days to come.
Strength and honor are his calling cards;
 serving God his greatest pleasure.
Meet him at the door with a kiss and a "Welcome home," ladies,
 for he is to be valued above diamonds,
 season tickets to the symphony—
 yea, even dark chocolate.
Festoon his plate with nachos and salsa;
 adorn his feet with cushions and turn on the game.
For fame is fleeting and hair color may fade,
 but a man who loves his family and his God
 is a living celebration.

33

What a Mom Makes

 My mother once said to me, "I hope you never get one of those tattoos. They're permanent, you know. But have children. Lots of children." So I did. And I have some news for you: Children are permanent.

The one thing he didn't explain is my mother's life. And until he can explain my mother's life, I'll stick by my mother's God.

**UNIVERSITY STUDENT TO A FRIEND
AFTER HEARING AN ATHEIST LECTURE**

When our kids were small, I learned some things. I learned to always look in the oven before turning it on. You never know what will be in there. You never know *who* will be in there. I learned that the Darth Vader LEGO character will successfully pass through the digestive tract of a three-year-old. I learned that when you hear a flushing sound followed by the words, "Uh-oh," it's too late. Do something else. I learned that a ceiling fan is not strong enough to rotate a 38-pound boy wearing Batman underwear and a Superman cape, but it will rotate a birthday cake fast enough to leave icing on all four walls.

Ramona laughed when I told her this years ago, but not as heartily as I had hoped. This surprised me. She is normally upbeat. The neighbor from whom you borrow. The one who stops and asks about your dog or your day. But lately the perkiness had vanished. She didn't kick the cat or scramble eggs on my head at breakfast, but the laugh was gone when I told her one of my impossible-to-resist jokes.

"What's wrong?" I asked.

She reminded me of the dinner we had enjoyed a few nights earlier with couples we admire. The ladies were comparing stress and jobs and shifts and hours worked, when one asked Ramona, "What do you do?" Our kids were young at the time. She had decided that if at all possible, she would be at home while they were. There she did the bookkeeping for our small business, chauffeured young children around, and served as fashion and homework consultant, chef, referee, life coach, personal stylist, economist, travel agent, encyclopedia, and CFO. But what came from her mouth was this: "I'm just a mom."

There was an awkward pause. So one of the guys filled it. "How much do you make?" He was joking, of course. We laughed.

"She makes me mind," I said, which was neither true nor all that funny, judging from the velocity of the punch I received upon my shoulder. So I tried changing the subject. "I'll tell you what *I* make. I make trouble."

Later Ramona lamented, "I don't how my friends do it. They're amazing. I don't have a degree. After the kids are gone, I won't have a high-paying job. Sometimes I wonder if I made a wise choice."

So I sat down and came up with a list for her. A list of what she makes.

- I make 1,000 meals a year—give or take a few hundred. 60,000 if you count the ones I make for our kids' friends.

- I make the children do the dishes, then shut off the TV and go outside so they'll learn something useful.

- I make threats but never idle ones.

- I make good on my promises.

- I make the kids apologize and hope they mean it.

- I make our house a home—one where the kids love to bring their friends. A place of peace. A place they're safe.

- I make them go to church in hopes it'll stick, in hopes they'll want to go all by themselves one day.

- I make their friends put their phones in a box when they eat with us. If they don't, I threaten to put their phones in the blender. One day I'll plug it in.

- I make them question easy answers, clichés, and wrong thoughts about heaven.

- I make them respect others by showing respect myself.

- I make them read books, pull weeds, and bathe the dog.

- I make them stop playing virtual sports so they'll play real ones.

- Sometimes I make pies from scratch. Sometimes I make excuses. And sometimes I make a beeline for the bathroom, where I lock the door and read a book.

- Most of the time I make myself very clear when disagreeing with my husband.

- I make time for owies, scrapbooks, and tea with friends.

- I make grass stains and boredom disappear.

- I make leftovers edible.

- I make vacations fantastic.

- I make mistakes—and ask for forgiveness.

- I make our children see that hard work is good and money is useful, but relationships make life rich—especially a relationship with the one who made it all.

- I make beds and coffee and payments. I make a difference.

- I make pickles; I make do; I make friends; I make up; I make out.

- I may not make much money, but I make footsteps worth following.

- I make my husband feel like a million bucks.

- Somehow I make time each day to sit and read the Bible and pray. It's making me increasingly aware that I'm valuable not because of what I make, but because of who made me.

- The God who loves me has made me a daughter of the King.

34

Why I Go to Church

 I have good news and bad news. The good news:
Costco now sells caskets. The bad news: To get one,
you have to buy twelve.[1]

On the most elementary level, you do not have
to go to church to be a Christian. You do not have to
go home to be married either. But in both cases if
you do not, you will have a very poor relationship.

R. KENT HUGHES

once asked my father, "If God wants me happy, why do I have
to sit through church?" We were riding in our rust bucket of a
Mercury Meteor station wagon at the time. It lurched. It limped.
And whenever my dad shut the ignition off, it kept running until he
kicked a front tire just right. I was seven or eight, which means I was
closing in on my eight hundredth Sunday church service.

Dad looked at me in the rearview and said something like, "This
is a big old car, Son. It's not always comfortable in here, and it could
use a few more air fresheners with five kids in it and all. But she gets
us where we're going—with or without you in it. Kinda like the
church."

I had no idea what he meant, and I'm not sure he did either. But
I smile now to think of it.

Children still have questions and thoughts about church and God. Here are notes they've written to their pastors:

> My mother is very religious. She goes to play bingo at church every week even if she has a cold. *Annette (I am 9)*

> Please say in your sermon that Peter Peterson has been a good boy all week. *Sincerely, Peter Peterson*

> I know God loves everybody, but he never met my sister. *Arnold*

> I'm sorry I can't leave more money in the offering plate, but my father didn't give me a raise in my allowance. Could you have a sermon about a raise in my allowance? *Love, Patty*

> I would like to go to heaven someday because I know my brother won't be there. *Stephen*

> Please say a prayer for our Little League team. We need God's help or a new pitcher. *Thank you, Alexander*

> My father says I should learn the Ten Commandments. I don't think I want to because we have enough rules already in my house. *Joshua*

> I hope to go to heaven someday but later rather than sooner. *Love, Ellen*

> I think a lot more people would come to your church if you moved it to Disneyland. *Loreen*[2]

Some Sundays I think, *More sleep would be nice. There's football on. The lake beckons. The fridge is right there. Church? Whatever for? We're swimming in online options. I can listen to the greatest preachers over a lazy breakfast. Besides, there are hypocrites at church. People who disagree with me. And what if the sermon goes into extra innings?*

So why do I find myself lacing up my dress shoes each Sunday? Why do I *want* to go to church—*need* to go to church? Is it because a Pew Research study from more than 20 countries says churchgoers are happier than those who don't attend?[3]

No. I think John Stackhouse nails it when he writes, "Church wakes us from the confused dimness of our busy routines and says, 'Don't forget! Don't forget God, and salvation, and the love of Jesus, and the companionship of the Holy Spirit and the world to come!'"[4]

Can't I do this just as well on the golf course? A better question is, "Do I?" The answer is no. I'm too busy hooking and slicing and slamming my club into the ground. I golf a lot. Trust me. People seldom worship there.

And so, we join with an imperfect bunch that meets each week. When someone hurts, we hurt—enough to do something about it. "We don't attend church," our pastor says, "we *are* the church." In time, our three children found friends and a home there. They discovered that a few people at church are grouchy; most are gracious. That's life.

One day the craziest thing happened: I stopped thinking of others seated near me who badly needed to hear from God, and I heard from him myself. I heard that I'm not here to consume but to contribute, not to be served but to serve.

I go to church because I cannot think of anything more important to do with two hours on a Sunday. I go because I need to encourage and be encouraged. To be accountable. I go to church because I need to connect with people who are very unlike me. I need the young guy updating me on chemo treatments. The old guy with the respirator. I need to hurt, and pray, and do something when I discover that someone has no family this Christmas.

I love one-on-one time with God. But there's nothing quite like watching my favorite sports team live or my favorite band in concert. In the same way, I long for what happens at church. Christianity, you see, is a team sport.

Our kids are long gone from the nest, and by God's grace, they go to church now too. Not because we tell them to but because, like me, they want to. Each of them has stood with me at Niagara Falls, in awe of the vast body of water, the culmination of a thousand tiny streams and rivers that empty into Lake Ontario through Niagara. It is a reminder of the power of seemingly insignificant people joined together with a common purpose.

So join us at church this week.

Please don't wait for the hearse to bring you there.

35

Stories Worth Telling

My friend is on a fairly restrictive diet. He only eats
coconuts and bananas. He hasn't lost any weight
yet, but boy, can he climb a tree.

Whatever your problem is, the
answer is not in the fridge.[1]
MARK WENSLEY

When a friend goes on a diet, I have always been of the opinion that it should not cost me money. But that was to change when over lunch, for the first time in world history, Steve Biggerstaff ordered a salad. "Are you okay?" I asked. "Have you taken ill? Shall I call someone?"

My British buddy laughed and stated the obvious: "I'm on a diet."

Now, please understand, I liked Steve the way he was. You wouldn't recruit him for your track team, but put this guy on the line in a football game, and opponents cringe and cower. They leave the field. They find other stuff to do. The guy is skyscraper tall. His arms are the length of my legs; his wrists are the circumference of my thighs.

Some, God made fast. Steve, God made big. I like it that way. I feel safe when Steve is with me. He's an ex-military guy who has guarded, among others, the queen.

"How much weight do you aim to lose?" I asked.

"A hundred pounds."

His words made me grin at the sheer implausibility of them. I'd seen him try this before. "Tell you what," I said. "I'll give ten bucks to our radio ministry for each pound you lose." He stopped nibbling on julienned carrots and blinked. "There's one condition," I warned. "You must donate ten dollars to the ministry for each pound you gain."

He dwarfed my hand in his and shook it. A little too excitedly.

"Well, look at this," I said. "The dessert menu. I'm paying. Aha! Butterfinger Cookie Dough Cheesecake." Steve shut the menu without blinking.

A week later, I mailed him some chocolate bars. He can't resist chocolate bars. But his wife, Sheila, said he wouldn't touch them.

"Can I pay you to leave little boxes of macadamia nuts smothered in chocolate around the house?" I asked her. "I fear this may cost me money."

"Sure," said Sheila. "Send some. I'll eat them; he won't."

And she was right. Steve kept eating his dainty salads, riding his little treadmill, drinking his carbonated water. He told me he liked this new lifestyle. His knees felt better. His heart felt better. His everything felt better. He laughed and told his wife, "I'm being paid per pound, you know." Still I knew I would have the last laugh.

Six months passed. Steve wasn't half the man he used to be. But his doctor said, "Keep going." And he did.

One day I was asked to speak on a Caribbean cruise. Sometimes God calls and I say, "Here am I. Send me." As a bonus, Steve and Sheila came along.

Though surrounded by an endless buffet, Steve ate the allotted calories each day. "Quick," I said, pushing an overflowing ice cream cone toward him. "Finish it. It's melting." He didn't balk. I ordered room service for him. Nothing worked.

To date, Steve's new way of looking at things has cost me $800.

It's worth every penny. He looks great. Feels great. Ask how he did it, and he'll smile. "One step at a time, brother. One 'no' and then another. It's a lifestyle, I suppose."

Steve's words remind me of my spiritual life. For too long I thought of sharing my faith like I'd think of a diet. I'd get all excited about it after some TED Talk or book or sermon. I'd tell others about Jesus, but I likely did more harm than good. On the Annoyance Meter, I ranked high. After one or two discouraging days, I was back at the same old buffet, loading up on pork chops.

Steve has me thinking there's a better way. Call it "diet-style" evangelism, if you will. What if we simply took small steps? Woke up and thanked God for another day to bring joy to others? Asked him at breakfast to help us be faithful? Read a few words from the Bible and did what they said? Took an active interest in neighbors, coworkers, and complete strangers on subways and airplanes? What if we were so completely overwhelmed by the love God has lavished on us that we passed some along? What if we showed extravagant grace—the kind we've been shown? What if we had more memorable conversations?

Quintin Stieff has been my friend for half my life. Over dinner one day he told me how he found himself talking with a complete stranger. The two hit if off from word one. Mostly, Quintin listened. Then the stranger asked, "What do you do?"

"I'm a pastor," he said.

The man flinched and stepped back a foot. "Oh, then you wouldn't like me."

"Why not?"

"Well, because I'm an atheist, and I'm gay. Now what do you think of me?"

"Two things," said Quintin. "First...I don't think you believe this yet, but I believe God created you in his image. That he loves you, and this gives you infinite dignity, value, and worth. And secondly, Jesus told me to love my neighbor as I love myself. And so I love you."

The man was speechless for a moment.

Finally, he leaned forward and asked, "Where is this church?"

The church is in Iowa. Quintin has seen it grow from a handful of people to four large services each weekend. How? One right step at a time, he would say. By God's grace.

Few people we meet need another finger in their face, but who can resist one who listens and cares? One who takes the next right step? Then another? May we be known by our love. When we are, we can't help but leave footsteps worth following—and stories worth telling.

Feel free to write and tell me your story. Why not throw in some chocolate? I promise I'll pass it along to Steve.

36

Not My Lipstick

 I didn't make it to the gym today. That makes five years in a row.

A four-year-old said, "Mom, what happens when you die?" The mom answered, "You go to heaven." The four-year-old said, "No. I mean when you die, do I get your stuff?"

When our son Jeff was 18 he came home and said to Ramona, "I want to get married, Mom. But I'd like to bring home three girls, and you have to guess which one it is."

Sure enough, the next day Jeff brought three beautiful girls through our front door and sat them on the sofa, where they began to converse with my wife. Finally, Jeff said, "Okay, that's enough, Mom. Guess which one it is."

Ramona didn't skip a beat. She pointed right at the one in the middle. "Her!"

"Wow," said Jeff. "How did you know?"

She said, "Because I don't like her."

It's not true. We love this girl very much. In fact, we have prayed for her from the time the two of them were small. And now that they're married with children of their own, we love to go to their place and do things they once did at our house. Like leave lights on everywhere. Doors open. Taps dripping. Best of all, we like to sit on their sofa late at night. Turn on some oldies. And neck.[1]

One of the keys to good relationships with your children's spouses is to make sure you refrain from writing about them without ample warning. So, with Raelyn's permission, I'd like to tell you a story about her. One of my all-time favorites.

It was a Tuesday afternoon in August when Raelyn found herself in a mall buying, among other things, lipstick. She tossed it in her purse and headed to her car, minding her own business, unaware that a stranger was lurking in the shadows. She must have looked like an easy victim. Petite. Wearing high heels and a dress. Listening to music through earbuds. Texting. Carrying a purse. Suddenly, before she had time to blink, that purse was seized from her shoulder by a man who took off running.

Now, you should know that although Raelyn is petite, she's also a farm girl. Just five foot three and 110 pounds[2], she once shot a moose. On purpose. I have seen her smack a golf ball 200 yards. And wrestle steers. And play defensive back and wide receiver in a women's tackle football league—which had the team motto, "You're tougher than you think." And she is.

The poor purse snatcher might have opted for another victim had he known any of this. But he jogged ahead of her, a happy crook, likely thinking, *She's got high heels. This is a breeze.*

But fast as you can say, "Hey!" Raelyn kicked off those heels and sprinted after that purse like she was launched from a steer. The poor guy barely knew what hit him. She tackled him from behind, slamming him down on the pavement.

"You broke my arm," he screamed.

"You stole my purse," she hollered.

Then she grabbed it from him. And hit him with it.

When Raelyn called to tell me what happened, I was in shock. So was her husband, Jeff. "Don't ever do that again," he told her. "What if…Well, so many things could have happened."

Raelyn agreed.

"What were you thinking?" I asked her.

She laughed. "It happened so fast," she said. "All I could think of was, *You're not getting my lipstick.*" And he didn't.

"Did you break his arm?"

"No. I don't think so."

"I bet he didn't tell his friends about this."

Raelyn laughed. "The purse probably didn't go with his outfit anyway."

The story hit the front page of the city newspaper.[3] "In football, I hit girls twice my size, and I take them down," she told a reporter. "It was a clean football tackle. I got a good wrap on him and put my arm below his waist. It was just a football tackle like in any game."

During the next week I told this story while speaking, and both times the crowd applauded. A few of the women stood. Perhaps it's because they've had quite enough of being hurt and robbed when they should be honored and respected. Perhaps it's nice to see someone stand up and say, "Not today. Not on my watch. Not with my purse."

Raelyn doesn't necessarily recommend doing what she did, but there is deep within each of us a longing for a place where justice is meted out, where people are no longer belittled and abused, where those we love dwell in safety and peace, home free. Perhaps Raelyn's story provides a brief glimpse of a day that's coming when wrongs will be set right.

Until then, we pray for these kids of ours out there in this crazy old world. May they look to God for help. Especially if they decide to tackle crime on the street.

37

The War Is Over

> My brother said that when I grow up I should be one of those guys at the circus who gets shot from a cannon. He said you get two bucks an hour plus traveling expenses. I said, "I wanna be a garbage man. They only work Wednesdays."

Happiness turns up more or less where you'd expect it to—a good marriage, a rewarding job, a pleasant vacation. Joy, on the other hand, is as notoriously unpredictable as the one who bequeaths it.

FREDERICK BUECHNER

One of my favorite sitcoms is undoubtedly *Hogan's Heroes*. When my daughter won the complete set at a golf tournament, we got little else done for about a week. We grinned at the buffoon Colonel Klink and laughed at the inept 300-pound sergeant of the guard, Schultz.

This sitcom, which ran from 1965 to 1971, was set deep in German territory in a fictional POW camp for captured Allied airmen. The Nazis, of course, are made to look like bumbling doofuses. The prisoners can leave and return almost at will via a network of secret tunnels. Radio contact is kept with the Allied command based in

London and code-named "Papa Bear." The incompetence of the camp commandant, Colonel Klink, doesn't hurt, and of course Schultz is always aware that the prisoners are carrying out mischief, but deliberately ignores it on constant threats of being banished to the Russian front.

As you might suspect, the show was controversial. Many felt it trivialized the suffering of real-life POWs. Ironically, the actors who played the four major German roles were all Jewish. They had faced discrimination and anti-Semitism and responded not just with dignity but with a great sense of humor. Part of the key to coping amid life's horrors, my World War II–veteran father showed me, was to find a way to laugh.

Rabbi Reuven Bulka believes that humor is one of the most effective ways of confronting adversity, especially when we have little control over it. "By laughing at our fate," he explains, "it is as if we were stepping out of a situation and looking at it from a distance."

In Jewish humor, tragedy and comedy are often inseparable. Much of it reflects the history of a people determined to stay alive despite overwhelming odds. One Jewish joke shared by Reuven Bulka tells of a Jew living in Russia who falls into a lake, and, unable to swim, screams, "Help, save me!" His calls go ignored by the soldiers. So he yells, "Down with the czar!" The soldiers instantly jump in, yank him out of the water, and take him to prison.[1]

In a real German prison camp near the end of World War II, American captives built a makeshift radio, risking severe punishment—even death—to receive welcome news broadcasts from afar. One day came the glorious news that the German high command had surrendered, ending the long and bitter war that had seen an estimated 60 million die.

Unfortunately for the German guards, a communications breakdown kept the news from reaching their ears. As word spread swiftly from prisoner to prisoner, a loud celebration broke out. As hope dawned, they began to sing. They waved at the confused guards, laughed at the German shepherd dogs, and shared jokes over their meager meals. On the fourth day, they awoke to find that all the guards had fled, leaving the gates unlocked.

The war was over. The time of waiting had come to an end.

We have all spent time imprisoned by difficulty. When people found out that we lost five immediate family members in one year, they graciously asked how we survived. Laughter helped, of course. But far better, we sunk our teeth into the unchanging promises of God. In particular, these words offered healing and hope:

> We're not giving up. How could we! Even though on the outside it often looks like things are falling apart on us, on the inside, where God is making new life, not a day goes by without his unfolding grace. These hard times are small potatoes compared to the coming good times, the lavish celebration prepared for us. There's far more here than meets the eye. The things we see now are here today, gone tomorrow. But the things we can't see now will last forever.[2]

For now, we see things imperfectly, like blurry reflections in a mirror. "We're squinting in a fog, peering through a mist. But it won't be long before the weather clears and the sun shines bright! We'll see it all then, see it all as clearly as God sees us, knowing him directly just as he knows us!"[3]

Don't get me wrong. I haven't found easy answers. But I have found hope. It comes from the belief that a better day isn't far from here. A day when all my question marks will be straightened into exclamation points. A day when, to paraphrase sergeant Schultz—I will see *everysink*.

38

Outrageous Claims

 A friend claims he can run the 400-meter dash in 16 seconds. I told him that's impossible. He said, "I know a shortcut."

I know of no one fact in the history of mankind, which is proved by better and fuller evidence of every sort to the understanding of a fair enquirer, than the great sign which God has given us, that Christ died and rose again from the dead.

THOMAS ARNOLD

was ten when my paternal grandfather showed me his homing pigeons. We drove them about eight miles from his house and let them go. They never came back. I've had years to think about this, and here's what I think: Those weren't homing pigeons at all. Those were just regular pigeons.

Have you ever believed something, then found out it wasn't true? Here are some far-fetched claims written on insurance forms.

"A house hit my car."

"In an attempt to kill a fly, I drove into a telephone pole."

"I had been driving for forty years when I fell asleep at the wheel and had an accident."

"The car in front hit the pedestrian but he got up so I hit him again."

"I was on my way to the doctor with rear end trouble when my universal joint gave way causing me to have an accident."

"I pulled away from the side of the road, glanced at my mother-in-law and headed over the embankment."

"The guy was all over the road. I had to swerve a number of times before I hit him."

"The pedestrian ran for the pavement, but I got him."

Isabel Parker pretended to slip and fall 49 times in various locations. She filed insurance claims totaling millions. Sadly for Isabel, her insurance company didn't *fall* for it.

Nor did Cracker Barrel when a Virginia woman claimed to have found a mouse in her soup. Inspectors agreed that the mouse had not been cooked or drowned in the soup. The scam was not a *Gouda* idea.[1]

But that doesn't come close to the claims made by North Korea's oppressive former leader Kim Jong Il.

Records reportedly claim that he learned to walk at three weeks and talk at eight weeks. He supposedly grew up to write more than a thousand books and six operas in three years. When he first picked up a golf club, it's said he shot a 38–under par round with 11 holes-in-one. Each of his 17 highly impressed bodyguards apparently verified that story.[2]

One day on a beach in Hawaii, a man approached my wife and me and said, "I'm Jesus."

"It's so nice to meet you," I told him, reaching out my hand. "Have you been raised from the dead?"

He blinked twice then said, "Yes."

"Can you bring me some friends to verify this?" I asked. "I'd love to talk to them." He blinked again and walked away.

Surely the most outrageous claim ever is that of Easter. That Jesus, God's Son, died, was buried, and then was raised to life. If it is false, Christianity is a lie. If it is true, it is the most compelling, transforming, and life-giving truth in history and we dare not laugh it off or ignore it.

I grew up in a Christian home, yet I had serious doubts about the faith. I lay awake many nights, hoping it was true and daring myself to look into it. Finally, I did. And though I have questions still, I cannot deny the sheer weight of archaeology and the compelling clues for the truth of the resurrection.

Most scholars agree that the letters of Paul were written and read just 20 to 30 years after Jesus' death. In one of them are claims of eyewitness accounts that the risen Jesus appeared to him (1 Corinthians 15:8) and to "more than 500 of his followers at one time, most of whom are still alive" (verse 6).

How could he possibly get away with this unless it were true? Only Jesus had followers who went to their graves because they insisted he had been resurrected. Why would they do this unless they had seen him risen?

At my father's graveside service a very strange thought hit me: *If God were to raise my dad from the dead, what would it take to convince people that it happened?* I live in a town of 3,500. Could it be done? Absolutely not—unless it were true. If you doubt me, try faking a resurrection where you live. Let me know how it goes.

Several times my wife and I have been privileged to visit the Garden Tomb in Jerusalem. On one occasion our guide smiled as he told us, "Three hundred thousand people a year visit this place to see something that isn't here." Outside the tomb is a wooden sign: "He is not here—for he is risen."

For the believer, there is no greater reason for joy. There is no better reason to laugh like a kid again. We are forgiven. Amid the heartache and pain in this temporary place, God has defeated death and promised us eternal life through simple faith in his Son.

I am sometimes criticized for laughing too much, but the truth of the resurrection makes it impossible for me to stop for very long. It is quite simply the greatest punch line ever. A holy God loves us. Surely this is the most outrageous and transforming claim in all of history.

39

What Billy Taught Me

 My uncle passed away. All he left behind was a cuckoo clock. So we shouldn't have much trouble winding up his estate.

A keen sense of humor helps us to overlook the
unbecoming, understand the unconventional,
tolerate the unpleasant, overcome the
unexpected, and outlast the unbearable.

BILLY GRAHAM

When I heard that Billy Graham passed away at the age of 99, I recalled the time many years ago when my assistant poked her head around the corner. "George Beverly Shea is on the phone," she said.

I laughed. "That's Billy Graham's soloist."

"I know," she replied.

If given the choice to visit the Pope or Mr. Shea, my parents would have picked the famous singer. Many mornings I awoke to his baritone voice singing, "I'd rather have Jesus than silver or gold." I was smart enough to know that the voice on the LP wouldn't be the voice on the other end of the phone.

I picked it up and said, "Yeah, right, Vance. What do you want?"

Silence. Then a deep baritone laugh. "Laughter is a good gift," he said, as we talked. "It's helped our team through many trying times." I thanked him for that laugh, but far more, for modeling integrity through the years.

When I first began traveling and speaking, temptation was a schoolyard bully. Never far away. Like the lure of a fishhook, it zipped past in the murky water. Without knowing it, Billy Graham became a long-distance mentor to me.

Billy knew about the lure of money.

In the late 1950s, NBC offered him a million a year to host a show. During a citywide campaign, a cynical press grilled him on finances and asked if he expected to mine substantial money from the city. Billy pulled out a telegram from Hollywood. It was a lucrative offer to star in two movies. "If my interest was in making money," he smiled, "I'd take advantage of an offer like this."[1]

Lyndon Johnson once told Billy before several staff, "I think you ought to run for president when I'm finished with my term. If you do, I'll put my entire organization behind you."[2] Texas billionaire H.L. Hunt even offered him $6 million to run for president.[3]

"Billy never changed his calling," said Ravi Zacharias. "Many times it could be said, 'God loved him and others had a wonderful plan for his life.' But he kept his focus."[4]

"I've never seen a man in my life that cared as little about money as Billy Frank Graham," said his younger brother Melvin. He also knew that money had great power to accomplish great ends.[5]

Billy knew about the lure of pride.

He was movie-star handsome with piercing blue eyes. Between 1955 and 2017, he won a spot on Gallup's roster of "Most Admired Men" an astounding sixty-one times.[6] Presidents and royalty welcomed his friendship and counsel. Yet he learned early on that if you put a guy on a stage and tell him he's wonderful often enough, he may start thinking he is, rather than thanking God. So he wrote, "The first thing I am going to do when I get to Heaven is to ask, 'Why me, Lord? Why did You choose a farmboy from North Carolina to preach to so many people?'"[7] He repeatedly gave credit to God for any good that came from his ministry.

Billy knew about the lure of immorality.

He made himself accountable, knowing it was a lie that temporary pleasure brings lasting joy. Even his critics admired him for it. And he had plenty of them. Those who accomplish anything worthwhile make mistakes. But he was quick to ask forgiveness, express regret for things said and done, and treat failure in others with kindness and grace.

As a direct result of his example, particularly his Modesto Manifesto[8], I asked friends to help me establish guardrails. As I read a "manifesto" Billy and his associates constructed, three sentences jumped out at me:

> We will be accountable, particularly in handling finances, with integrity according to the highest business standards.

> We will tell the truth and be thoroughly honest, especially in reporting statistics.

> We will be exemplary in morals—clear, clean, and careful to avoid the very appearance of any impropriety.[9]

For me, this has meant being brutally honest with and accountable to close friends like Wayne, who looks me in the eye and says, "Cut the baloney, Callaway. Tell me the truth."

It has meant never being alone with a woman other than my wife.

It has meant avoiding environments where it's easy to fall.

It has meant that I don't travel alone. Sure, it costs money—and for some this is impossible. But when I began taking my wife or my kids along, everything changed. And it's surprising how many friends you have when you offer them a trip somewhere.

It has also meant living a thankful life. We simply cannot leave footsteps worth following if we're characterized by ingratitude. We need to be thankful on a daily basis for God's grace. Thankful that there's more joy in the light than in the dark.

Billy Graham knew about joy. He once told of the man who got up to preach but wouldn't stop. He rambled on for an hour and 20 minutes. The guy who introduced him couldn't stand it. Finally he picked up a gavel and threw it at the speaker. It missed the speaker and hit a man in the front row. Before blacking out, the man said, "Hit me again, I can still hear him."[10]

When Billy passed away, Twitter was awash with a quote attributed to him. But the words were actually written by D.L. Moody many years earlier. I picture the two of them having a little laugh over it in heaven. Surely the quote summarized Billy's life and ministry too.

"Someday you will read or hear that Billy Graham is dead," said the Twitter quote which was shared every 15 seconds that day. "Don't you believe a word of it. I shall be more alive than I am now. I will just have changed my address. I will have gone into the presence of God."[11]

One day I plan to look up that address and thank Billy for practicing what he preached. Heaven is looking sweeter all the time.

Runaway

 My dad once told me that he thought of running away, but by the time he got his teeth in, found his glasses, and located his car keys, he forgot where he was going.

Only when our greatest love is God, a
love that we cannot lose even in death,
can we face all things with peace.

TIMOTHY KELLER

When I was four or five my older brothers wouldn't let me join their football game. So I skulked around the sidelines a little. This didn't work, so I decided to run away. Before leaving, I informed my father of my plans. He said, "Here. I'll help you pack." That pretty much took the gas out of my tricycle.

Through the years unhappy children have left runaway notes for their parents.

"Dear Mom and Dad. We ran away because we think you and Dad need a break from us. We always will love you both. Don't worry about us. We have food. Please don't look for us. We'll come back tomorrow at 7:00 am, I promise. It's also a break for us. Love always: Kristy, Theresa, Matthew, Samantha."

"Mom, I'm going to run away tomorrow at 9:30 when you and Dad are sleeping. Be sure to say goodbye forever. Emily. P.S. I will be packing tonight."

"Dear Mommy, your trobles will to be gon soon. I will run awy tomoro so you can have a better life without me."

In the early 1920s the Soviet Union embarked on a fateful journey, running away from God, seeking a better life by becoming the first state whose ideological objective was to eliminate religion and replace it with universal atheism.

Ten years later, the brutal dictator Joseph Stalin gave orders that were carried out with a vengeance. Religious property was seized. Believers were ridiculed and harassed, then sent to prison camps. Atheism was propagated in the schools.[1] In one account, children were ordered to pray to God for candy. The children prayed. When nothing happened, they were told to pray to Stalin. When they did, candy rained down upon them.[2]

When the empire finally struck out in 1991, *The Jesus Film*, thought to be the world's most viewed movie, aired for the first time in Russia. Upon seeing it, a government official came to faith in God and ordered sweeping changes to the educational system. Millions of Russian children began to hear the good news of God's love in state-run schools.

In the city of Stavropol, Russia, Doug and Kyle Clarkson worked with a team of teachers who wanted to base their curriculum on biblical principles. They handed out Bibles but soon ran short. Someone mentioned that Bibles confiscated by Stalin in the 1930s had been stored in a warehouse outside of town.

One member finally summoned the courage to go and check it out. Arriving at the warehouse he asked the officials, "Is this where Bibles were stored?"

"Yes."

"Are they still here?"

"Yes. There are thousands of them."

"Can we remove them and give them back to the people of Stavropol?"

"Yes."

The next day they hired some of the locals, took a truck to the warehouse, and began loading up. One of the workers was Dimitri, a college student who had come only for a day's wages. He was an agnostic.

Halfway through the job, Dimitri disappeared.

"Have you seen him?" someone asked.

No one had. So they went looking.

In the corner of the warehouse, they found him. He was holding a Bible and weeping. Composing himself, Dimitri finally explained that he had decided to steal the Bible. But when he opened it, he was unprepared for what he found inside.

"Here," he said, flipping the Bible open and showing them the first page. "That's my grandmother's signature."[3]

This grandma and her grandson were separated by decades, but it seems like her prayers had finally been answered. Though she was long gone, her godly life had not stopped speaking. Her grandson was stunned at the lengths God had gone to reach him. He had run far from his grandmother's footsteps, but not far enough to outrun the good shepherd, whose arms were open wide.

41

Closer to Home

 I was sitting on a plane when the guy beside me said, "Look at those people down there. They look like ants." I said, "They are ants. We haven't taken off yet."

If you read history you will find that the Christians
who did most for the present world were
precisely those who thought most of the next.

C.S. LEWIS

This past week I flew across the country. I slept in four hotels, visited five towns, and hopped on six flights. I delivered seven speeches, ordered ten restaurant meals, and ate twenty-three little bags of pretzels. I rarely leave home without my wife, but this week I did. I sometimes tell people that when I travel without her, I shave one leg. That way, when I climb into bed at night, it feels like she's right there beside me.

But it's not true. When I climbed into bed each night, I was fully aware that she wasn't with me. Fully aware I was far from home.

There's a file of songs on my phone titled "Home." So I found myself singing duets with people like John Denver and Ian Thomas and Gerry Rafferty.

Home.

When the final flight touches down, I have it down to a science. I'm a carry-on-luggage-only kind of guy. I sit as close to first class as I can. Squeeze past stragglers on the gangway. Stride down the escalator two steps at a time. Sprint to my car, praying for green lights and no speed bumps. I speed just a little (ten percent for a tithe), scanning the horizon for the lights of home. The gal who loves me is there. My own bed. My own fridge.

Home.

We all long for it. Check the country charts if you doubt me. Hundreds of hit songs have been written about it. "The Green Green Grass of Home." "My Old Kentucky Home." I count twenty-one songs all titled simply, "Home."

One of my favorite songs of home is from Carrie Underwood. She sings of a six-year-old orphan boy who's used to loneliness. He's been shuffled from house to house, from school to school. New moms. New dads. New houses that will never be home. When people ask him how he likes his new place, he smiles and says, "This is my temporary home."

Underwood sings of a young single mom searching for work, looking for love, longing for hope. At night the mom reassures her baby girl that this stop at a halfway house is only temporary.

Underwood sings of an old man in a hospital bed surrounded by people he loves. "Don't cry for me," he tells them, "I'll see you all someday." The years have shown him that even the most opulent of earthly homes is a temporary stopover on the journey to his final destination.

I've sat by that hospital bed. Said goodbye to parents who were passing through. What promised to be enduring was so brief. You don't meet older folk who say, "It's just gone so *slow*." When my dad died, a friend said, "I'm sorry you lost him." But I hadn't. I knew where he was.

The book of Revelation rattles us with graphic battles and fiery pits and dragons. And smack-dab in the middle of it we encounter earth-shattering hope. John writes of that day when God's home will be among his people. "He will wipe every tear from their eyes, and there will be no more death or sorrow or crying or pain. All these things are gone forever" (Revelation 21:4).

No more death or pain? That's right. No more soup kitchens, orphanages, or funeral homes. No first aid, no Band-Aids, no hearing aids. No dentist offices, police stations, or divorce courts. No anxiety or depression. No worry or fear. What would you give in exchange for a home like that?

A little girl lived close to a graveyard. One dark night a friend was walking her partway home. "Aren't you afraid to go through the cemetery?" the friend asked.

The little girl laughed and said. "No. See those lights? My home is on the other side."

Heaven awaits those who have trusted Jesus as Savior. We leave footsteps worth following by making a difference in this world while longing for the next one.

Each flight, each pretzel, each song takes us one step closer to home.

42

Floods of Joy

Our kids came fast. The anesthetic from the first birth was still working for the third. Someone asked what's it like to have 3 kids in 3 years. I said, "We're far more satisfied than the guy who has 3 million dollars. How so? Well, the guy with 3 million wants more."

If God does what you think he should do, trust him. If God doesn't do what you think he should do, trust him. If you pray and believe God for a miracle and he does it, trust him. If your worst nightmare comes true, believe he is sovereign.

CRAIG GROESCHEL

Have you wondered, *Where is God? What is he up to?* Sophie does. She is four now and brave, but already she wonders. Just yesterday a huge hardcover book jumped off a shelf and landed on her tiny foot. On the way to the ER she watched her foot turn three shades of blue. Her mother took pictures and sent them to me. It was a nasty gash.

"Mom," Sophie said as they sat in the waiting room, "I wish Jesus wasn't invisible so he could come and hold my hand."

Me, too, little girl.

David Flood knew the feeling. In 1921 he and his wife, Svea, left Sweden to take the good news of Jesus to a remote area of Africa. The chief said, "No," so they built a mud hut nearby and prayed for a breakthrough. None came.

Twice a week a boy came to see them, hoping to sell them chicken and eggs. They bought some, and Svea told him of Jesus, the God who would rather die than live without him. The boy prayed a prayer, but that was it. Pregnant, Svea endured malaria, gave birth to a little girl, and died.

Her grieving husband, David, dug a rough grave and buried his 27-year-old wife. Handing his daughter to another missionary couple, he announced, "I'm going back to Sweden. I've lost my wife. I can't take care of this baby. God has ruined my life."

The little girl grew up in South Dakota. Her parents named her Aggie. Aggie married and gave birth to two children.

One day a Swedish Christian magazine showed up in her mailbox. She had no idea where it came from. But a photo caught her eye. A grave. A white cross. And the words *Svea Flood*.

The story was from long ago. It was about missionaries. The birth of a baby. The death of a young mother—*Aggie's* mother. And one little African boy she had led to Jesus.

The boy had grown up and built a school. Gradually, he won all the students to faith in Jesus. The chief too. There were 600 Christians in the village now, all because of what God had done through Aggie's parents, David and Svea Flood.

For their twenty-fifth wedding anniversary, Aggie and her husband were given a vacation to Sweden, where Aggie learned that David Flood had remarried, fathered four additional children, and given his life over to alcohol. "Don't mention God," she was told. "He hears God's name, and he...well, don't."

In a rundown building, Aggie found her father—the one-time missionary. Seventy-three now, he suffered from diabetes. Cataracts covered both eyes. Aggie fell to his side, crying, "Papa, I'm your little girl, the one you left in Africa."

"I never meant to give you away," he said. "I just couldn't handle things."

"It's all right, Papa. God took care of me."

He stiffened. "God forgot us all."

"Papa," Aggie continued, "you didn't go to Africa in vain. Mama didn't die in vain. The little boy you brought to the Lord grew up to win his whole village to Jesus. The one seed you planted kept growing and growing. Today there are at least six hundred African Christians because you were faithful. Papa, Jesus loves you. He never hated you."

David Flood broke. Tears of sorrow and repentance flowed down his face, and right there he prayed, recommitting his life to Jesus.

Within a few weeks, he was gone.

Years later, Aggie and her husband attended a conference in London. A report was given from the Congo area, where Aggie had been born. The speaker represented 110,000 believers. Afterward, Aggie approached him and asked, "Have you ever heard of David and Svea Flood?"

His eyes grew wide.

"Yes, madam. Svea Flood led me to Jesus when I was a little boy."

In time, Aggie and her husband visited her birthplace, where they were welcomed by throngs of villagers, and Aggie was escorted to her mother's grave. There she knelt before that white cross and gave thanks.[1]

I don't pretend to understand the ways of God. That would be like an aardvark understanding the internet. But when I heard that story for the first time, I needed it so badly. Needed to know that in the midst of my hurt, anxiety, and mess, an all-powerful, sovereign God was working things together for good. Needed the reminder that he is active, that he cares.

Do you feel abandoned? Do your prayers seem to bounce off the ceiling? Please don't give up. Seeds you are sowing now will bear fruit one day. Maybe not this week or even next year. But through it all you have a God who entered our world and suffered. A God who weeps. He will not waste this hurt. He is in the midst of whatever you're up against. In even this, God is sovereign.

Jesus is "sustaining all things," says Hebrews 1:3 (NIV).

"No human wisdom or understanding or plan can stand against the LORD," Proverbs 21:30 tells us.

"I am God, and there is no other," says Isaiah 46:9 (NIV).

"My counsel shall stand," Isaiah 46:10 (ESV) tells us, "and I will accomplish all my purpose."

I cannot run the world, but God can. I don't pretend to understand it all, but he does. I cannot quite see it from here, but it's true: Heaven's throne is occupied. And all is well.

With Sophie's foot finally bandaged, her mom drove her home. Suddenly, my granddaughter started to laugh. "Jesus is making it not hurt as much as it should," she said. "Jesus gave me you, Mommy. You hold my hand."

Jesus holds your hand, too, little girl. Never forget. Hold on tight.

Waytago

Twenty-six years ago I penned my first book for Harvest House Publishers. Many of the same energetic and gifted people who helped orchestrate that book worked on this one. Thousands of blessings to Terry Glaspey, who believed in this little eight-ounce ambassador, Bob Hawkins Jr. who led the charge, Betty Fletcher and Kim Moore who attempted to keep them in line, and Barb Sherrill whose contagious laugh I can hear whenever things get real quiet and I think about it. As if they weren't enough, there's Brad Moses, Hope Lyda, Gene Skinner, Sharon Shook, and Carmen Meyers. It is good for a man to hang out with those who are wiser than himself.

To Stephen, for invaluable assistance in writing—and for giving me grandkids.

To Rachael, for calling me Daddy all these years. And giving me grandkids.

To Jeffery, for laughing like a kid all your life—and…you get the idea.

To Ben and Deb Lowell, for sharing my dream of spreading joy. You are visionaries, friends, and laughers.

To Steve and Sheila Biggerstaff. I owe you chocolate. You know why.

To Pat Massey, my loyal assistant these 29 years. You are gracious, long suffering and, I'm sure, very tired.

To James Enns, a fine historian and loyal friend.

To my eight grandchildren, who landed here in just over three years. We love you, Aaron, Caleb, Claira, Eowyn, Judah, Macy, Seth, and Sophia. Methinks grandchildren are even better than actual children.

To Ramona. Thirty-seven years ago you said you would. And you have. I still find myself driving too fast whenever I'm coming home. It's your fault. Despite seemingly insurmountable odds, you've filled our house with peace, joy, and chocolate desserts that are a foretaste of heaven. God bless you, my girl. Let's grow old together. Oh wait, we already have.

Notes

Lighten Up a Little

1. Another joke which lit up my inbox: When our kids were small, we loved seeing that beautiful sign at Comfort Inn. Have you seen it? "Kids stay free." We would just drop ours off. "Here, you take 'em. We'll be back a week from Tuesday."

   Now, for the record, we love our kids. We would give our lives for our kids. Except for our youngest. (I'm kidding! We love our youngest.) We have never left him behind anywhere. Ask him. I don't think he's even stayed at a Comfort Inn. Maybe he's afraid of going near one after hearing this joke.

What Tornado?

1. The Canadian Press, "Man Who Mowed Lawn with Tornado Behind Him Says He 'Was Keeping an Eye on It,' " *CBC News*, June 6, 2017, http://www.cbc.ca/news/canada/calgary/three-hill -tornado-lawn-mower-1.4145466.

2. Ashifa Kassam, https://www.theguardian.com/world/2017/jun/05/canada-lawnmower-man -tornado-theunis-wessels.

3. Adam Boult, *The Telegraph,* June 5, 2017, https://www.telegraph.co.uk/men/the-filter/keeping -eye-says-father-mowed-lawn-tornado/.

4. "Der Chuck Norris des Rasenmähens" [The Chuck Norris of lawn mowing], *Spiegel Online*, June 6, 2017, http://www.spiegel.de/netzwelt/web/rasenmaehen-bei-tornado-das-web-feiert-theunis -wessels-a-1150714.html.

5. Peter Holley, "The Lawn-Mowing-in-a-Tornado Dad Photo That Inspired a Thousand Memes," *The Washington Post*, June 5, 2017, http://www.washingtonpost.com/news/capital-weather-gang /wp/2017/06/05/the-lawn-mowing-in-a-tornado-dad-photo-that-inspired-a-thousand-memes/.

6. "Man Who Mowed Lawn," *CBC News*.

7. Barry Fontaine, Twitter post, June 3, 2017, 11:56 p.m., http://twitter.com/BFMediaPro/status /871259240094081025.

Nine Minutes to Live

1. Psalm 46:1-2 NIV

2. According to *HuffPost*, online pornography viewing in Hawaii cratered during those 38 minutes (77 percent below the average) when people thought this was the end. It then spiked afterward (48 percent above the average) when people discovered they weren't going to die after all. How would you spend your time if you had nine minutes left?

   Josh Butler, "Hawaii's Porn Usage Tanked After Missile Alert, Though It Spiked Later," *Huff Post*, January 17, 2018, http://www.huffpost.com/entry/hawaii-porn-missile-alert_n_5a5fed 79e4b054e351771eab.

The Fear-Driven Life

1. Bill Bryson, *The Life and Times of the Thunderbolt Kid* (Random House, 2006), 197.

2. "Timeline," *Bulletin of the Atomic Scientists*, http://thebulletin.org/doomsday-clock/past -statements.

Water Has Broken

1. Verses 4-7.

Wrong Number?

1. John 3:16 and Ephesians 2:8-9.

Big Hairy Deal

1. @SadderDre, Twitter post, September 1, 2014, 4:19 a.m., http://twitter.com/SadderDre/status /506400839439622144.

2. @SadderDre, Twitter post, September 1, 2014, 5:09 a.m., http://twitter.com/SadderDre/status /506413422402359296.

Magnetic Personality

1. Jimmy Nsubuga, "Pet Hamster Stuck to Cage for Three Days After Eating Fridge Magnet," July 6, 2017, http://metro.co.uk/2017/07/06/pet-hamster-stuck-to-cage-for-three-days-after-eating -fridge-magnet-6759705.

2. Jonathan Edwards, "Christian Happiness," *The Works of Jonathan Edwards*, ed. Wilson H. Kimnach, vol. 10, *Sermons and Discourses 1720–1723* (New Haven: Yale University Press, 1992), 294-301, http://edwards.yale.edu/archive?path=aHR0cDovL2Vkd2FyZHMueWFsZS5lZHUvY2d pLWJpbi9uZXdkwaGlsby9nZXRvYmplY3QucGw/Yy45OjQ6MS53amVv.

3. Justin Buzzard, "Christian Happiness," *Justin Buzzard*, January 4, 2010, http://www.justinbuz zard.net/2010/01/04/christian-happiness.

4. Philippians 4:8.

Forbidden Smile

1. After leading an extensive study on our top fears, Dr. Christopher Bader, professor of sociology at Chapman University, said, "People tend to fear what they are exposed to in the media. Many of the top ten fears this year can be directly correlated to the top media stories of the past year."
   Chapman University, "What Do Americans Fear Most? Researchers Release Fourth Annual Survey of American Fears," *Phys.org*, October 11, 2017, http://phys.org/news/2017-10-americans -4th-annual-survey-american.html.

Mamma Mia!

1. Revelation 12:10 tells us that Satan is accusing us before God, day and night.

God and the Giant Veggies

1. Matthew 5:45.

2. Deuteronomy 30:9-10; Isaiah 48:18; Psalm 1; 2 Corinthians 9:8.

Miracle in Cell Block 3

1. Mark 12:43-44 NIV.

2. Viktor Frankl, *Man's Search for Meaning* (New York: Pocket, 1984), 86.

The Bad Old Days

1. Psalm 143:5 ESV.

2. Charles R. Swindoll, *Saying It Well* (New York: FaithWords, 2012), 180.

Oh, Leon

1. See Matthew 9:9.
2. See Acts 9:1-6; 13:9.
3. Verses 13-14.
4. Kevin Kaduk, "Leon Lett and Don Beebe Celebrate Twentieth Anniversary of Famous Super Bowl Play," *Yahoo! Sports*, February 3, 2013, http://sports.yahoo.com/blogs/shutdown-corner/leon-lett-don -beebe-celebrate-20th-anniversary-famous-200119844--nfl.html.

#Selfie-Centered

1. Tim Elmore, "Nomophobia: A Rising Trend in Students," *Psychology Today*, September 18, 2014, http://www.psychologytoday.com/ca/blog/artificial-maturity/201409/nomophobia-rising -trend-in-students.
2. "The average US adult will spend 3 hours, 43 minutes [a day]…on mobile devices in 2019, just above the 3:35 spent on TV."
   Amy He, "Average US Time Spent with Mobile in 2019 Has Increased," *eMarketer*, June 4, 2019, http://www.emarketer.com/content/average-us-time-spent-with-mobile-in-2019-has-increased.
3. "Americans are viewing their smartphones more often than ever before, on average 52 times per day."
   "Global Mobile Consumer Survey: US Edition" (2018 results), *Deloitte*, accessed August 16, 2019, http://www2.deloitte.com/us/en/pages/technology-media-and-telecommunications /articles/global-mobile-consumer-survey-us-edition.html.

Parenting Tips

1. Though I'm not sure who first said or wrote this, it is most often attributed to Erma Bombeck, who also said, "One thing they never tell you about child raising is that for the rest of your life, at the drop of a hat, you are expected to know your child's name and how old he or she is."

My Very Own Time Machine

1. See Isaiah 1:18.
2. Philippians 3:13-14 PHILLIPS.

Very Punny

1. Alfred Hitchcock, "Alfred Hitchcock—'Puns are the Highest Form of Literature,'" YouTube video, 1:51, from an interview by Dick Cavett in 1972, posted by "mountpilot," August 9, 2008, http:// www.youtube.com/watch?v=gu5g86nhWK4.
2. Dale Carnegie, *How to Win Friends and Influence People* (New York: Simon and Schuster, 2009), 56.

Makin' Carrot Biscuits

1. *Merriam-Webster*, s.v. "mondegreen," accessed August 19, 2019, http://www.merriam-webster .com/dictionary/mondegreen.
2. Jeff Aronson, "When I Use a Word…Words Misheard: Medical Mondegreens," *QJM: An International Journal of Medicine* 102, no. 4 (2009): 301-302, http://doi.org/10.1093/qjmed/hcp002.
3. Another child sang, "He's the champion out of Venice with the great Sir Arthur's sword."
4. The author of this song, Robin Mark, is notorious for telling me jokes. When I told him how one

child had heard his song, he laughed so hard I worried about him. The correct version, of course, is "Riding on a Cloud."

5. That's "peace like a river," child. Give peace a chance.
6. "I am a friend of God; he calls me friend."
7. "Open the eyes of my heart, Lord."
8. The preferred version is "Sunbeam."

"New" Steps to Happiness

1. Alexandra Sifferlin, "New Ways to Become Happier—and Healthier," *TIME* magazine, October 2, 2017, 31.
2. https://www.wired.com/story/our-minds-have-been-hijacked-by-our-phones-tristan-harris-wants-to-rescue-them/
3. Morten Tromholt, "The Facebook Experiment," *Cyberpsychology, Behavior, and Social Networking*, 19, no. 11 (2016): 661-666, http://dx.doi.org/10.1089/cyber.2016.0259.
4. Dan Evon, "Did Bill Gates, Steve Jobs, and Other Tech Billionaire Parents Advocate Limiting Children's Technology Use?" *Snopes*, August 30, 2018, http://www.snopes.com/fact-check/tech-billionaire-parents-limit.
5. https://www.theatlantic.com/magazine/archive/2017/09/has-the-smartphone-destroyed-a-generation/534198/
6. Markham Held, Amanda MacMillan, Alexandra Sifferlin, and Abigail Abrams, "New Ways to Become Happier—and Healthier," *TIME* magazine, October 2, 2017.

Lettuce Theology

1. See Galatians 5:22-23.

Seven Coincidences

1. "Four-Year-Old Lands on Feet After Falling from Third-Story Window," *CBS Denver*, March 3, 2013, http://denver.cbslocal.com/2013/03/03/4-year-old-lands-on-feet-after-falling-from-3rd-story-window.
2. Francis Collins, interview by Steve Paulson, "The Believer," *Salon*, August 7, 2006, http://www.salon.com/2006/08/07/collins_6/.
3. Chole, *Finding an Unseen God*, 138,172-173.
4. Ibid., 161.
5. Ibid., 154.

Leave Footsteps Worth Following

1. Psalm 90:12 ICB.

Daddy of the Bride

1. KJV.

The Proverbs 31 Dad

1. David Mikkelson, "Collect Phone Calls on Father's Day," *Snopes*, last modified June 21, 2015, accessed August 21, 2019, http://www.snopes.com/fact-check/we-love-you-mdash-call-collect.

Why I Go to Church

1. I didn't make up the first part of this joke. Costco sells caskets online, one at a time. I'm dead serious.

2. The sources for these quotes are unknown. Although my source is a thick file I keep marked, "Kids. Funny."

3. Joey Marshall, "Are Religious People Happier, Healthier? Our New Global Study Explores This Question," *Fact Tank*, Pew Research Center, January 31, 2019, http://www.pewre search.org/fact-tank/2019/01/31/are-religious-people-happier-healthier-our-new-global-study -explores-this-question.

4. John Stackhouse "Seriously, Go to Church," *Faith Today*, July/August 2018, 46.

Stories Worth Telling

1. Whatever your question is, the answer is not in this footnote. I saw this line on a t-shirt some-where but was unable to find the source of it. My good buddy Mark Wensley is pretty funny, so why not him?

Not My Lipstick

1. My parents used this term a lot. It's an ancient term for smooching. The first time my daughter heard me employ it, she said, "That's anatomically weird." She was correct.

2. In the interest of my own health and wellness, I received Raelyn's permission to tell you this.

3. "Lethbridge Herald Newspaper Archives," Newspaper Archive, May 24, 2012, accessed July 2, 2019, http://newspaperarchive.com/lethbridge-herald-may-24-2012-p-1.

The War Is Over

1. Leo M. Abrami, "Laughing Through the Tears," *My Jewish Learning*, accessed August 22, 2019 (orig-inally published in *Midstream* magazine), http://www.myjewishlearning.com/article/laughing -through-the-tears.

2. 2 Corinthians 4:17-18 MSG.

3. 1 Corinthians 13:12 MSG.

Outrageous Claims

1. Beverly N. Williams, "Mother Gets Year in Mouse Soup Case," *Daily Press*, July 6, 2006, http://www.dailypress.com/news/dp-xpm-20060706-2006-07-06-0607060299-story.html.

2. Amanda Morrow, "Kim Jong Il: Top Ten Weird Facts About North Korea's Late Dictator," *PRI*, December 19, 2011, http://www.pri.org/stories/2011-12-19/kim-jong-il-top-10-weird-facts-about-n -koreas-late-leader.

What Billy Taught Me

1. Harold Myra, Marshall Shelley, *The Leadership Secrets of Billy Graham* (Grand Rapids: Zondervan, 2005), 67.

2. Ibid., 68.

3. Ibid., 68.

4. Ibid., 67.

5. Ibid., 107.

6. "Billy Graham on 'Most Admired' List for Record Sixty-First Time," *Billy Graham Evangelistic Association*, December 27, 2017, http://billygraham.org/story/billy-graham-on-most-admired-list-for-record-61st-time.

7. Billy Graham, *Just as I Am* (New York: HarperCollins, 1999), 723.

8. "On This Date: The Modesto Manifesto," *The Billy Graham Library*, October 24, 2017, http://billygrahamlibrary.org/on-this-date-the-modesto-manifesto.

9. Harold Myra, Marshall Shelley, The Leadership Secrets of Billy Graham (Grand Rapids: Zondervan, 2005), 61.

10. https://billygraham.org/story/the-lighter-side-of-billy-graham/

11. https://www.christianitytoday.com/ct/2018/february-web-only/billy-graham-viral-quote-on-death-not-his-d-l-moody.html.

Runaway

1. "Anti-Religious Campaigns," *Revelations from the Russian Archives*, Library of Congress, August 31, 2016, http://www.loc.gov/exhibits/archives/anti.html.

2. https://books.google.ca/books?id=Z00EAAAAMBAJ&pg=PA30&lpg=PA30&dq=%22pray+to+stalin%22&source=bl&ots=8vwm7-s35b&sig=ACfU3U1CnQKir7hUYzH1xf_9UEDlZbOiww&hl=en&sa=X&ved=2ahUKEwjd9pmzorPlAhX8HDQIHYg4By0Q6AEwDHoECAkQAg#v=onepage&q=%22pray%20to%20stalin%22&f=false.

3. Luis Palau with Mike Yorkey, *It's a God Thing* (New York: Doubleday, 2001), 50-52.

Floods of Joy

1. James Collins, *Tears in My Heart* (Xulon Press, 2007), p. 310. https://books.google.ca/books?id=SYIrIzhnrEMC&pg=PA310&dq=david+and+svea+flood&hl=en&sa=X&ved=0ahUKEwjxvLLIprPlAhXKGDQIHdpFCF0Q6AEIXjAH#v=onepage&q=david%20and%20svea%20flood%20svea&f=false.

About the Author

Phil Callaway is the bestselling author of more than 25 books. He hosts *Laugh Again*, a daily radio show and podcast that airs on stations throughout North America and in England, English-speaking Africa, the Caribbean, and Australia (laughagain.us, laughagain.ca).

He speaks for corporations, conferences, and churches on marriage, faith, and learning to laugh in tough times. Phil's other books include *Under Par, Tricks My Dog Taught Me (About Life, Love, and God), To Be Perfectly Honest, Family Squeeze,* and *Laughing Matters.*

To check out his books, CDs, and DVDs, or to find out more about his ministry and connect with him, visit Phil at:

www.philcallaway.com
twitter.com/philcallaway
facebook.com/philcallawaybooks

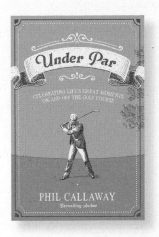

Heart and Humor That Are Far Above Par

Hit the links with popular humorist and golf enthusiast Phil Callaway as he shares stories of friendship, faith, and failure he found while on the fairway. From tee to green and all points in between, join Phil in a celebration of one of the world's most exhilarating and exasperating pastimes.

Aim for the flag as you enjoy anecdotes such as…

The Itch—A long Canadian winter does nothing to stop some dedicated and determined early risers.

The Backyard Classic Scarcity and ingenuity give birth to the Airport Golf and Country Club, a unique course with 18 fairways and only one green.

Escape from the Hanoi Hilton—A prisoner of war passes time and wins the battle for his mind.

Prayer on a Golf Course—Will one man's wish for an elusive hole-in-one be granted by God?

Fore Is Short for Forgiveness—A dangerously errant drive leads to a lesson in mercy.

Packed with unforgettable quotes, helpful tips, and amusing asides, *Under Par* will inspire you to never give up on the game you love…even when it doesn't love you back.